in his own wo

Bono

Susan Black

OMNIBUS PRESS
London / New York / Sydney

Copyright © 1997 Omnibus Press
(A Division of Book Sales Limited)

Edited by Chris Charlesworth.
Cover & Book designed by Michael Bell Design.
Picture research by Nikki Russell.

ISBN 0.7119.5299.X
Order No.OP47797
Visit Omnibus Press at http://www.musicsales.co.uk

Exclusive Distributors:
Book Sales Limited, 8/9 Frith Street, London W1V 5TZ, UK.
Music Sales Corporation, 257 Park Avenue South, New York, NY 10010, USA.
Music Sales Pty Limited, 120 Rothschild Avenue, Rosebery, NSW 2018, Australia.

To the Music Trade only:
Music Sales Limited, 8/9 Frith Street, London W1V 5TZ, UK.

Photo credits: Harry Goodwin: 26,63b; London Features International:
front & back cover, 4,6,8,9,10,12,13,14,15,16,18,19,20,22,23,24,25,27,30,32,
35,36,38,41,42,44,45,46,47,49,50,51,52,53,54,55,56,57,58,59,60,62,63t,
64,65,66,67b,68t,70,72,73,75,76,78,79,80,81,84,85,88,89,90,92,93,94,96;
Rex Features: 28,37,68b,86; Peter Stone: 31,67t,69,74,82.

Every effort has been made to trace the copyright holders of the
photographs in this book but one or two were unreachable. We would be
grateful if the photographers concerned would contact us.

Printed in the United Kingdom by Page Bros. Ltd., Norwich.

A catalogue record for this book is available from the British Library.

Introduction

U2 are the most successful band Ireland has ever produced.
Van Morrison might have created more myths, Thin Lizzy may have
had more hits, the Boomtown Rats possibly told journalists
better stories, but not one of them ever had the same impact,
the same emotional energy and rode the same wave of commercial
momentum as U2. Almost from the moment the band arrived in
England, four bewildered teenagers from Dublin with nothing more
than a brace of native hits behind them, Bono, the Edge, Larry
and Adam were catapulted into the spotlight, first as musicians,
then as songwriters, then as people.

**U2 is a democracy, there is no leader of the band, there
is no accepted spokesman within its ranks. But to most people,
the people who buy their records, who attend their concerts,
the face of U2 is the face of Paul Hewson, the charismatic singer
who prophetically Latinised his own future reputation when
he rechristened himself Bono Vox – Good Voice, Great Voice.
Now he is better known simply as Bono, but the implication is
still there, and still true.**

Bono was born on 10 May 1960 in Dublin. He grew up
in Ballymun; he remembers it today as a rough neighbourhood,
"a high tower block area with gangs running loose." He grew up
there, but he spent more of his time in the mythical Lipton Village
with sundry friends. It was surely more than coincidence that
the village's most notable inhabitants went on to form two of the
most exciting bands Ireland has ever produced; U2 on the one
hand, the Virgin Prunes on the other.

**"Lipton Village. It's an imaginary place, somewhere we
developed in our imaginations to give us an alternative lifestyle
as kids. We grew up studying people on street corners.
We laughed at the way they talked and at the expressions
they made. We mocked the adult world and agreed we would
never grow up because all we saw was silliness."**

Bono was 17 when U2 formed at Mount Temple, Ireland's
first comprehensive school. The four members' interest in music
was nurtured and fostered by the attentions of their teachers.
At first the group played cover versions alone, but according to
the Edge, the ideas behind the band were already firmly in place.
The band was simply a means of expressing those ideas.

**U2's story is Bono's story. But Bono's words are not
necessarily U2's words. The band say what they need to in
their songs – their lyrics are their mouthpiece, and reflect all
they see, feel and believe. When they give interviews, much of
what they say simply reiterates what the songs say, amplify
those sentiments, perhaps place them into contexts which the
music might not wholly represent. But they talk about a lot
of other things as well, things that mean a lot to them, to their
fans and to the world. And of them all, it is Bono who has
said the most. He isn't necessarily the most talkative member,
but he is the most talked to. He sings, therefore people expect
him to speak as well. And of course, he agrees.**

Throughout it all, however, he remains intensely personal.
And the media respect that, just as it respects the honesty and
integrity which has almost become U2's trademark. In concert,
he gives everything he has, and then some more on top.
And when he talks, he leaves no stone unturned there, either.

The Band

Bono On Bono

It's the easiest thing in the world to be cynical. I can see it coming in myself sometimes and I have to stamp it out. You see it all the time. *February 1981*

I remember watching *Top Of The Pops* and seeing this group called Middle Of The Road singing 'Chirpy Chirpy Cheep Cheep'. I must have been about 8 at the time and I thought, 'Wow! This is what pop music is about. You sing like that and you get paid for it.'. *February 1981*

When I was 16 I couldn't cope with the idea of getting a job, getting married, growing up and dying – I wanted more and I fought to break out of that rut. In the Sixties you had this love and peace movement where people were rebelling against the standards and the hypocrisy of their parents' lives, and they broke out of that. And I think they were right. I'm into that rebellion, it's just that that rebellion was diluted by escapism, through drugs.

That's how, if you like, the world dealt with it, calmed it down. And with punk it's the same thing. Tribalism, another form of escapism. I like to think of our music as a celebration, just breaking down those barriers. *February 1982*

I grew up without a record collection. My brother had tapes of people like Free and Hendrix. Last time I was in London I wanted to get some soul music; I went into Rough Trade and felt very embarrassed because I didn't know what to ask for. *February 1982*

I don't care what people are, whether they've long hair, short hair or they're skinheads. If someone is being excited by the music, then I'm happy. I don't care for clichés myself, or stock responses, but people get a chance to let go at our gigs and they do it. As long as it's not violent or too alcoholic – and by that I don't mean being drunk, but becoming senseless – if people express themselves then that's good. And if élitist followers are put off by that then that's up to them. *January 1982*

What I'd like to see is people burning the rule books... the rule books that say they have to like this sort of music and nothing else. I think people should broaden their vision... there's some great music happening on ethnic fronts, like African music, and I'm particularly interested in Irish traditional music. At the same time, I'm sure there are some great pop songs, but I want more out of music than just that. I want music with the X factor, music with that heart and soul.

I don't want to sound pretentious, truth is a two-edged sword, it cuts deep. I can tell when a singer is singing what's in his heart and when he isn't. There's a big difference, and there's a lot of glossy pop songs that can maybe make us cry, but it's a bit like watching *Lassie* or *The Little House On The Prairie*, you know, it's not real emotion, it's a kind of thin level of emotion. The truth is when a singer starts saying something that comes from right down within him, and it affects you right down within you, and that's when you start talking about great music, as distinct from nice music. *February 1982*

The word 'nice' is a horrible word... music for lifts, music for supermarkets. I think that's fine if you're going shopping or going up and down, but I want more than that. Is that wrong? Is it wrong to want more out of music? *February 1982*

What interests me are the three primary colours, guitar, bass and drums. The Moody Blues and the London Philharmonic Orchestra – well, is that rock'n'roll? The three sounds are basic enough to have unlimited resources. *February 1982*

Without sounding (like) a total idiot, I can't remember being bored over the last ten years. An hour on my own is just so special to me. I just don't get bored, there's too much happening. *February 1982*

What I want from music are people who lay themselves on the line. People like John Lennon or Iggy Pop did that. Whatever you feel about their music, you do learn about them from it. If anything, that's where the divide lies. *February 1983*

When I talk about love I'm thinking of unselfish love. Sex can be bought and sold just like anything else. But I think real love is about giving and not expecting anything in return. *February 1983*

I think if there's a difference between the art and the artist there's something up. *November 1984*

I think because of the spiritual side of the group that I was associated with, people thought 'this is dangerous.' That this guy believes in what he's saying because rock'n'roll is all a 'shirk and a shrug'. And of course, I'm not into rock'n'roll for that, I'm just not, and I think that made people uncomfortable. In Ireland the two things you shouldn't talk about are politics and religion and we did. *November 1984*

I talk too much. I don't talk too much when I'm with people that I believe in and they believe in me. *November 1984*

Humanness is what I'm interested in, not being superhuman or subhuman. There's as much fear on our records as there is faith. Maybe we've walked ourselves into it. Our first record we had a boy's face on the cover, the whole perversion-of-the-innocents thing. Maybe we've dug our own grave. That was just one of the dimensions of it. I, more than any other member of the group, have been responsible for digging the bigger hole. *January 1985*

I don't consider anybody to be plain. I think a lot of the vanity that is rock'n'roll at the moment is just people afraid to look at themselves in the mirror. They're afraid of what they might see and so they just kind of cover it up. I'm talking about videos, the whole thing. Rock'n'roll's just skin deep at the moment. There's not a lot of soul music being made in 1985. I hope there will be in 1986. I'm an optimist. *May 1985*

I think the music is much better than the musician, but also the audience is as much applauding itself as us. One of the things people forget about these large concerts is that the audience have heard the records, it knows the songs from the radio and the music has become part of their lives. When they hear those songs their own selves are caught up in them and they are in some way applauding the connection. *June 1985*

I warn you, I am completely unable to explain myself at times... even to string three words together can be hard, and this can be

tragic if people think you supposedly have a gift of the gab. These days I feel like I've got less and less to say. Something's happened that kind of changed my point of view, which is that I've really got interested in this idea of the song... It's like out of the air, with a guitar or piano and three or four chords, you just say all you have to say and it's incredible. It's just something that never even dawned on me before... I'm a songwriter, why don't I shut up! *June 1985*

I met Elvis Costello a few months back and he said to me, 'I'm ambivalent about U2, I love it and I hate it.' He said, 'You walk this tightrope that none of your contemporaries will walk – they're afraid to walk it – and when you stay on I bow my head, but you fall off it so many times' and... there was no answer to that. We do fall off, a lot, and on stage I'll try for something and it won't work and... but it might work and that's the point, it might work. *June 1985*

I use our songs to wake myself up. It's like sticking a needle in your leg after it has gone to sleep. *January 1986*

Rock'n'roll is obsessed with sex in the back seat of a Chevrolet. Now, I'm sure sex in the back seat of a Chevrolet is pretty good for those involved, but I'm more interested in writing about relationships past that point. I'm interested in the mental conflict of a relationship. A lot of our songs are rooted in that. People have said that I'm obsessed with borders and I suppose I am, although it has never been something conscious. But there can be a lot of different kinds of borders – physical, national, sexual or spiritual, and there are elements of them all in U2 songs. *March 1987*

I guess I'm just an over-the-top guy. The Irish are great dramatists. The English hoard words and the Irish spend them. We're loose. Like James Brown, 'I'm a sex machine'. Now, that's not subtle. On one level we're accused of being too subtle and on another, we're not subtle enough. *March 1987*

I want to be a singer. I aspire to being a soul singer. My heroes are Van Morrison, Janis Joplin... but on the other hand they're Scott Walker and Elvis Presley... and trying to work in the two is where I am at the moment. The other interesting thing is that all the people that inspired me when I was growing up all had the same confusions about faith and fear of faith. Bob Dylan, Van Morrison, Patti Smith, Al Green, Marvin Gaye, this has been a real encouragement to me. *March 1987*

If I am an icon I think I must be a very bad icon. People mistake the music for the musician. What's special about U2 is the music, not the musician. I and the others are just ordinary people and our trade is to make music. Somebody else's is to build houses or work in a factory or teach. We're just getting to grips with our trade as songwriters. *March 1987*

Everyone argues, then we do what I say. *March 1987*

I don't think I'm a good singer, but I think I'm getting to be a good one. On 'Unforgettable Fire' I think something broke in my voice and it's continuing to break on 'The Joshua Tree', but there's much more there. At the end of 'Unforgettable Fire' Eno said, 'Bono has given me enough to get away with it, but he hasn't given me all he's got.' I've given him more on this record, but there's a lot more to come. I know that. *March 1987*

When I hear U2 records I hear my voice and I hear an uptightness. I don't hear my real voice. A lot of it was to do with writing on the spot, making them up as I went along. But Chrissie Hynde said to me, 'If you want to sing the way you think you want to sing and the way you can sing, then write words before you sing.' I'd never done that. I was literally writing the words as I was doing the vocals. I thought writing words was old fashioned. A hippy thing to do. I thought what I was doing in sketching away was… Iggy Pop had done it and he was a bit of a hero. I thought that, as soon as I had a pen in my hand, I was a dangerous man. *March 1987*

I'm loosening up a lot as a person, about my position in a rock'n'roll band, about U2. But for years I really wasn't sure about who I was, or who U2 were or, really, if there was a place for us. Some people say that U2 are self-righteous… but if ever I pointed a finger I pointed it at myself. I was defensive about U2 and therefore I was on the attack. *March 1987*

I break out in a cold sweat at the thought of drawing out money. It's bureaucracy. Whether to choose the blue slip or… those kind of decisions are impossible! Going to a supermarket nearly gives me a breakdown! I can write three verses for a song sitting in the bath, but Post Offices make me go weak at the knees. *December 1987*

**I see the value of being irresponsible at the moment.
There are people who would like me to stand and point them in
the right direction, and I'm just not going to do that. I'm a singer
in a rock'n'roll band. It's absurd to expect me to do anything
else. Yet, such is the vacuum left by the religious people and
political men now, that they look to people like Bob Geldof for
an idea on how to solve world hunger! Isn't that absurd?
December 1987**

Where's my public? My God, they've deserted me! This is a crisis.
We'd better do something. Stir up some publicity or something.
'Bono in under-age sex orgy.' That should do it. I want my public
back. *December 1987*

**You only get disillusioned if you had illusions to begin with.
December 1987**

I am still learning about the trappings of stardom. I just punched
a security guard over there and it felt pretty good. I'm wondering if
someone could bring me a bottle of Jack Daniels so I could drink
it in front of you. *At a press conference, 1987*

**There's no stage big enough for me – I like to stretch the
stage, to push it to its limit. I'm always trying to get across –
to communicate.**

Money has never had anything to do with how rich I feel.
All money has done is remove me from my friends and family which
are my lifeblood. It's cut me off.

**I mean, what's my motivation? *On making movies,
February 1988***

I've got a book... I've written poems but I don't know if I'll publish
them. If I do I'll call it *Fuck Off! Volume I*. I get annoyed when people
expect me to be a great all-rounder. *December 1988*

**It's just so great being in a rock'n'roll band it's very hard to do
anything else with your life. It's such a cliché, rock star can act,
so what? But then again we've done every other cliché,
might as well go for it.**

I make a certain type of music with U2 and I get pulled this
way and that and they'll say, 'Oh, Bono he's so serious, he is this
he is that.' Nobody says that about Coppola.

**I don't want to be the rock'n'roll star who's always giving
out about what he loves, because I do love it. I wouldn't do it if
I didn't.**

What's a rock'n'roll band? I'm not even sure if we are a
rock'n'roll band, but right now I'm enjoying pretending we are.
February 1992

**The biggest hit that you get, is when you're in the room.
Playing. And the music comes. And you don't know where it
comes from, and you don't know where it's going, and that's the
moment. And... that really pays your wages... February 1992**

My only responsibility is to be irresponsible. To tell people not to trust me. I'm a rock'n'roll star, that's what I do. I say, 'Don't believe a word I say!' I take the money. I run. And that's what people should know about me. *March 1992*

I am just a musician, and I don't know any more or any less than any guy on any bar stool – in any bar. I'm not a hero. I'm a rock'n'roller. I'm spoilt rotten. I'm paid too much for what I do. I'd do it for nothing, you know. You know what I mean? It's like – you people, you need heroes, you know. People want to... the media want to create heroes. But if I agreed to the job, you'd kill me! So, I'm backing out. *March 1992*

Never trust a man who tells you, 'It's from the heart.' You should know that. You should know that! Never trust a man who's smoking a cigar, second of all, never trust a cowboy, or a man in shades. Check this out (takes off sunglasses) – see – I'm learning to be insincere. I've had my bastard lessons. I'm getting it right. And finally – I could turn out cool. *March 1992*

I enjoy some of the more absurd sides of rock'n'roll, and I used to be shy of that. I used to kind of hide from it, and I was afraid that the bullshit would kind of overtake us – and it did! But now I think it's OK. You actually find out that you like some of the bullshit. I mean, some of it's fun. I mean, I would never do an interview in shades before, but now, you know, I'm learning to be insincere, I'm learning to lie.

People ask me such serious questions – and I answer them. I'm that dumb.

It's an amazing feeling, to be able to do what you want, when you want. And that is, you don't have to kiss ass, you know that feeling? There's a lot of people out there have to kiss ass every day, every week – just to make a, you know, a buck. Just to... and I don't. I have to kiss Edge's ass occasionally, maybe Larry, but you know...

Rock'n'roll is another language, and if you think about it like that it helps. I mean that's how I figured out how to listen to Michael Jackson – I just pretend I can't speak English and I'm a huge fan as a result. I mean that – I actually love the sound of his voice, the whole thing not just the lyrics. It's the man in the mirror that fucks me up. It's another language you're trying for 'A wop bop a looba a wham bam boom' or whatever it is.

I print the lyrics on the record sleeves because I don't think that as a singer I'm clear enough. There was a fantastic Japanese translation I have to tell you about of a song called 'Out Of Control.' I think the opening line – it's not great poetry but it was the opening line and I wrote it on my 18th birthday. I think it was 'Monday morning, 18 years, how long' and the Japanese translation was 'Monday morning knitting ears of gold...'

I think the world is not ready for a book of my poetry. I wrote a poem about Elvis. I think if you're going to write poetry it should be about Elvis.

If you are lucky enough to be in love as I am, you don't want to throw it all away and expose your partner: that is much more important to me than being in U2, actually. So when I'm writing songs, it's the leg of my experience, the arm of somebody else's.

But I do think that in an oblique way the only place in my life where I am completely honest is in the song.

I have written the odd tune on the back of an Air India sick bag.

I think there's nothing more radical or revolutionary than two people loving each other because it's so hard to do it and to keep those feelings going.

My father, who I love very much, is one of these guys who believes what he reads.

Well, the first thing to know about rock'n'roll lyrics is that they're not literature, they're something else, something more or less. The words are only part of the story and often what I have to do as a singer is to try to put words on the feelings and the atmosphere that's in the music. That's kind of what my job is.

In successful songs a lot of things are coming together, but it's not like I'm going to sit down and write a song called 'Miss Sarajevo', but that a tune will come, there's a mood to it. I try to figure out an image that fits that mood.

We got another good one from the Far East which was that I was doing a duet with Frank Sinatra called 'I've Got You Under My Chicken', which again is very much better. I might put that on my grave. A surrealist anthem.

I have at home an extensive library of classics, right the way through to books on gardening. I've thousands of books and I've read the first 17 pages of all of them (laughs). I don't know how much of this influenced our work, but I'm a fan. I'm simply a fan of these writers. I think the UK Year of Literature is great because I would like to believe that people still read.

I love and am a huge fan of Seamus Heaney and in fact there's a song on one of our earlier albums called 'A Sort Of Homecoming'... which was his. I guess I was trying to play with his style there a little bit. I love the literature of the place and am happy to take that, but not some of the other things. I mean, the music business in the UK is our spiritual home, that's what we grew up with, with all the Inkies and *Top Of The Pops* and *The Tube* and all that. It's kind of interesting because we were at this award show recently and a guy from *Q* magazine got up and made a very emotional speech about the band and I thought 'Wow' because having grown up with this but still sometimes to not feel a part of it, is funny, I think.

The first responsibility of a rock'n'roll star is not to be dull.

The Edge

A brilliant guitar player, but who completely understates it as a person. He pulls no shapes. He is a man of angles, he's got his chin and his guitar and the elbows and plays away and then humbly takes the plug out of the amplifier and goes home. My respect for him grows and grows. *May 1981*

I think that Edge is the head of the band, I'm the heart, and Adam and Larry are the feet. *May 1981*

When we started it was hard to get the Edge to play aggressively.
He is a gentleman and he plays guitar like a gentleman.
February 1982

**The Edge is a really, really intense guy, he's got this incredibly
high IQ, he's great at sorting out issues of worldly importance,
it's just that he forgets the everyday things, like the chords
of songs, where he is and so on. *January 1983***

Edge doesn't know a lot of the chords he plays. He makes them up.
They don't have names. *March 1987*

**There was a gig in America once when I threw Larry's drum
kit off stage and had a go at the band. And the Edge, who is my
ideal – he's completely composed – he was so outraged he
gave me a severe dig in the mouth. It was amazing. I've known
him all my life and it was a really good dig in the mouth. That
was on-stage... in front of Talking Heads and the B52s. I think
they all thought it was part of the show. *March 1987***

Edge is Welsh and a very proud Welshman. I fell in love
with a Welsh girl when I was 15 and she left me for a milkman.
She was probably right.

Adam

Adam stuck out like a sore thumb. *September 1980*

**Adam used to pretend he could play bass. He came round
and started using words like action and fret and he had us
baffled. He had the only amplifier, so we never argued with him.
We thought this guy must be a musician, he knows what he's
talking about and then one day we discovered he wasn't playing
the right notes, not one! *February 1981***

Adam is a very melodic bass player. He doesn't play the
usual lines. *February 1982*

**Adam Clayton... if it wasn't for Adam Clayton I wouldn't
be in U2. Adam Clayton found Paul McGuinness, our manager,
Adam Clayton booked our first gigs. I owe so much to him.
He's totally committed to being in U2. For a few years I didn't
know whether I wanted to be in a band and U2 didn't know.
We thought we might break up. It was after 'Boy', which I
thought was a great album. I lost interest. I had less interest in
being in U2 and more of an interest in other sides of me...
whether I was talking to a Catholic priest in the inner city or a
Pentecostal preacher I was sucking up whatever they had
to say. I was interested in that third dimensional side of me
and I thought rock'n'roll was a bit of a waste of space.
    I thought, okay, U2 were good at being a band, but maybe
we could be better at doing other things, real things like getting
involved in the inner city or something. Not just pointing out
the problems, but trying to sort them out. We were teetering on
the brink of collapse.
    Adam was completely heartbroken about this. He was
totally disillusioned because he was more interested in other
spirits like whiskey or tequila or anything else he could lay his
hands on. I'm all right now, I've come to terms with being in
a band... I think now this is what we do best. *March 1987***

Adam literally got me by the scruff of the neck and roped me into U2. I didn't really want to be in a band. I was only into it for the sake of the sound of electric guitar, drums, bass and singing. So when he started talking about actually playing gigs I thought, 'What, y'mean playing gigs in front of other people?' The thought had never dawned on me. But Adam believed in the band before anyone else did – he'd made up his mind at 15 or 16 that rock'n'roll was what he was going to do. *1988*

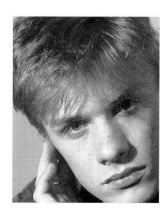

Larry

My earliest memory of Larry was when we were starting off. We were at our first rehearsal in his kitchen and all these girls, all these 14 and 15 year old girls kept climbing over the walls and looking in at the windows at Larry. Larry just shouted at them to go away and then turned the hose on them. He's not interested in being a pop star. Larry likes to play the drums. *May 1981*

A lot of people think the power comes from the guitar, but it's really from Larry's drums. *February 1982*

Larry is the core of U2. He never does interviews. He just gets on with his life the way he always has. He still enjoys being back home with his mates. *1987*

Beginnings

I was one of those kids it was impossible to tie down from
the very beginning. People used to – and family still do – put up
the cross (ie make a cross sign with their two fingers) whenever I
came in. They called me the Antichrist at age 8! *November 1987*

**We had these queues for miles and the cars just kept
coming so I quit.** *On an early job as a petrol pump attendant,
November 1987*

The idea was that we write our own material because we couldn't
really do anyone else's. That's the risk we took. At the start we were
criticised for using our own material, but we were making mistakes
whereas established groups weren't. They were taking the safe way
out… The only way to go is to make the mistakes. *December 1979*

**Even from the very start we wanted something like
the power of The Who and something that was as sensitive
as, say, Neil Young; you know how on edge he can be and
we always wanted that. Even though we couldn't really get it
together musically, there was something there and I call it
the spark. I called it something you must have. We've built on a
spark, we haven't tried to put the spark in our music. Like our
main influences in this group are each other. They're not outside.
They're very definitely each other.** *September 1980*

I remember thinking the first time we went into a rehearsal
that a movement was going to emerge that would be a breakdown
between flower power and the boot boy. I didn't really know what
I was saying, because it turned out to be punk rock. *February 1981*

**The most important thing about the beginnings of U2
is that we were four people before we were four musicians.
When we started out we couldn't play any instruments. We built
the band around the drum kit but when we were on-stage we
were a shambles. It was like every night we'd want to break up,
but then every morning we'd wake up and want to start again.**

I guess we did take ourselves too seriously, but our crime
was being seen to take ourselves too seriously. An interesting thing
about self-righteousness, belief is so unfashionable these days.
Whether it's belief in yourself or in something other… 'self righteous,
pontificating', these are the stones we throw at people who make
it through.

**I had the loudest mouth. When we formed the group I was the
lead guitar player, singer and songwriter. Nobody talked back at
first. But then they talked me out of being lead guitar player
and into being the rhythm guitar player and then they talked me
out of being the rhythm guitar player and into just being the
singer. And then they tried to talk me out of being the singer and
into being the manager. But I held on to that. Arrogance may
have been the reason.** *May 1983*

What really bothers me is that for two years, myself and Ali
lived in Howth, on the same road as Phil (Lynott), in a little cottage
that we rented at the time. And I would see him everywhere else
but on the street. Every time I saw him, he'd say, 'Why don't you

come down for a bite.' And I would say, 'You have to come up for a bite.' Every single time. And I never did call down and he never did call up. That's what came back to me. I never did call up.

Early on, where we'd play the Dublin Dandelion Market, or Belfast, or Cork... it was out of the '77 explosion we came, and the idea of being on-stage and being a star was something that us 16 year olds found repugnant. I suppose as a result of that I always felt when I was on-stage that I had to acknowledge that it was a little preposterous. So I'd end up in the audience. *March 1987*

When we started, the only bands who were making any money in Ireland were the showbands who played other people's songs. Of course, at one time – when there was only Irish television – people didn't know what Gerry and The Pacemakers and The Beatles looked like, so they would see these guys in red suits and painted on smiles and imagine that they were Gerry and The Pacemakers; that they were The Beatles. That was the tradition, and everyone rebelled against that.

But that anger has been replaced, by me, with a kind of affection, 'cos live music is bigger in Ireland than it is in any other country in the world: more people, per head of the population, go out to see a band and more people play instruments. So it's actually because of that tradition that the Irish are able to make money by being musicians. *1988*

It's almost impossible to be married and on the road, but Ali is able to make it work. A year went by when I hardly saw her at all. I was coming in when she was walking out the door. Still she's a very strong person and she doesn't take any shit from me.

The Creed

The name U2 is ambiguous, it's in-between… like the tightrope that we're treading. *June 1980*

We're looking for creative freedom. If we do make money we're looking for the fact that we can buy instruments and develop, nothing less. I couldn't care less about money. We've done without it for so long that at this stage it doesn't seem important. We're not thinking about getting married or bringing up kids, that isn't a relevant part of it. *June 1980*

U2 music seems to fill a space. It's not urban music, it's more to do with hills, rivers and mountains – and so it actually suits being outdoors rather than being contained in a club. *June 1980*

What can happen is that you turn just a circle instead of the spiral. We look at a spiral so that we can get higher. I look at it like a tower with people all round. If you're at the bottom, only the ones nearest can hear you. You've got to climb higher for those further back.
   It's just as important to reach those people, they might have heard less good music, they might have nine to five jobs. I think success and building it up is important. You must always climb. It can be a routine to climb, but I see it like a spiral, getting higher, or else it can be a circle where you're staying at the bottom, just touring/album making/touring/album making… *June 1980*

The overall thing we're dealing with at the moment is, we're 19, under adult status. There's a lot of people who've been around the business for years. They've lost that original inspiration from the adolescent years, the confusion. Out of that confusion comes a semblance of what you're trying to find yourself. It can be a very explosive time. So a lot of our songs deal with that sort of struggle. I use the image of twilight because it's neither dark nor day. It's grey, things are hard to see. There's much more confusion when you're at this age. You're fighting against it all the time. *June 1980*

Four people, four individuals, four friends, before they were in a band. It is important. I was saying about session men, these people who can get into a band without any real creative expression. They just want to get in there, they want it for the next big thing, blah blah blah. The most powerful music is created naturally. Is not forced at all. It just comes out. In London, a band grows, comes out, has its bash and if, in a year, nothing happens, they break up. We've been through that. If we were going to break up, we'd have broken up by now. *September 1980*

Music means a lot, but what some fans have not separated is the music from the musician. The musicians are just ordinary people. It's the music that's extraordinary if you like.

To be honest, U2 saved my life in a way because I'm literally unemployable. There's nothing else I can do.

We've seen and learned a lot already. It could leave us either cynical or with a determination and a spirit not to fall or go under. *February 1981*

I wouldn't say that we're bitter about rock'n'roll; we didn't enter this in a naive way. There are a lot of untruths in rock'n'roll, the word itself conjures up certain amoral standards to conform to and certain morals. But it's all superfluous imagery, it doesn't actually exist, that's not what it's like. Girls don't run around trying to rape people, you can't get drunk every night and do loads of drugs everyday. *February 1981*

U2 play with guitars, bass and drums on-stages and make records which go on radios, like anyone else involved in the music business. I see no real reason to say we're something else so we're going to play swinging from a chandelier tonight and that makes us different. It doesn't mean you're different. It means you're trying to be different. *February 1981*

Our biggest problem getting to a bigger audience is that we don't look a certain way, we don't fit into a little box. We're not a ska group or something that's easy to digest. But the fact that we're not easy to digest means we stick in the throat and a lump in the throat has far more guts to it. I believe ultimately... I don't know what I believe ultimately, but I know it's good that we're not easily digested. *February 1981*

I don't feel we've been hyped by the music press because I happen to agree with the good things they say about U2. The music press relationship with U2 has meant that a lot of people have come along expecting a lot but they've got a lot. If people come along expecting the world from U2, then they're gonna get it. I'm not scared we won't be able to give it to them. *February 1981*

I feel that we are meant to be one of the great groups. There's a certain chemistry that was special about the Stones, The Who and The Beatles and I think it's also special about U2. *October 1981*

We know what we are. What we have in this band is very special. The sound may be classical in one sense, but it's naturally our own. We don't sound like any other group. Our songs are different – they hold emotions of a spiritual nature. *February 1982*

There is a natural friction, a wonderful friction. I don't think our egos are self-egos; we've a band ego. I can say to the Edge, 'I don't like that thing you've just played' and he doesn't go, 'And I don't like what you've just done', he goes, 'You must be right otherwise you wouldn't have said it.' *February 1982*

A lot of bands digging into 'dangerous' areas do it in an obvious way. U2 don't need to do that. We can cover fear and love as part of a spectrum. *February 1982*

U2 is not about fashion. We don't want to be in fashion, because being in fashion is going out of fashion. *February 1982*

There is a stage where fashion becomes fascism. But I think people should always appear as they want. *February 1982*

U2 is just natural, we're really just four people – within ourselves we have a very strong relationship, like a love between

the band which spreads into the crew, our sound engineer, to the management, even to the record company, and then spreads into the audience. *February 1982*

Great music should be able to break through barriers, class barriers or whatever. *February 1982*

As a band we have a giant collective ego. It picks us up. Anyway, I don't think I'd be a good bank clerk. Or a hot dog salesman. I might be a good president. *February 1982*

We, as a garage band, believed you've got to be what you are and do what you want. Rebellion has to start within you. Our music may not bow down to your idea of what it should be. But it has to be respected as an individual view. A refusal to give up what you believe. *February 1982*

My attitude is 'So what?' We've still sold more records than most 'hit single' bands. We've excited audiences more. But the time may have come for us to sharpen our singles outlook. We have the melodies of a great pop band. But we don't have structures like that. Or hit singles. *February 1982*

I want to see the long-term effects of groups like ours and the Jam. Our emotions aren't just glossy throw away things. Some people saw 'A Day Without You' as escapism, but it was about suicide. I don't expect people to dig into our material with a knife and fork but… *February 1982*

We may well be the future of rock'n'roll, but so what? *March 1982*

Rock music can be a very powerful medium and if you use that to offer something positive then it can be very uplifting. On the other hand, if you use your songs to convey bitterness and hate, a blackness seems to descend over everything. *February 1983*

I think there is a certain insight in this group, a certain ability to see human emotions and expose them honestly. There are a lot of clichéd songs around in the chart. The fiction factory loves churning out superficial songs about the same old subjects. That's just something we refuse to do. This might sound egotistical, but I think we'll always retain our honesty. *February 1983*

We want a joust. The guitar, bass and drums set up is good for giving people a good slap in the face. We've chosen to work in that format even though a lot of people threw it out the window a couple of years ago. It suits us. We believe that passion is more important than technique. 1975 was all about style and technique. Herbie Hancock and jazz-rock, and 1982 was much the same with groups like Level 42. I believe we need that slap in the face that we got in 1976. The élitist thing has got to be smashed down again.

It's like Orwell's *Animal Farm*. The pigs have all become the farmers. The bands that were our contemporaries, the garage bands of 1976, are back on the big star trip. They're playing the part of the people they pulled down. It's either intellectual crap or patronising gloss. *February 1983*

**People see us as four guys who are uprooted from their
city of Dublin and thrown across the world. And we are winning.
We are beating the businessmen at their own game by
conquering the USA on our own terms. We might not be this
week's thing but that will never bother us.** *February 1983*

When you listen to U2 you are listening to the four people involved.
There's no mask. We are U2. *February 1983*

**The hope that's in the music comes from the hope that's in the
band. I believe it's time to fight back in your spirit – right down
deep inside. There is great faith in this group.** *June 1983*

Sometimes when we're song writing we get the feeling we're
actually channels for some creative thing that's happening. It's like
writers sometimes say it's in the air. They literally just pull things
down. *October 1984*

**I started reading the music press again recently, and I've
noticed there are two definite types of musician who talk to the
press There are people who say listen to this wonderful music,
aren't I great? And those that say listen to this wonderful music,
isn't it great? We are definitely in the latter.** *October 1984*

There is a danger in being a spokesman for your generation
if you have nothing to say other than 'Help.' That's all we say in
our music. It's never, 'Yes folks, here we go, here's the plan.'
It's always, 'Where's the plan?' *October 1984*

People charge us with being traditional and it gets up my
nose. Why are people so concerned about changing the face of
music, when the face is really only the facade? Like there's
Bruce Springsteen working within traditional American rock'n'roll
and he says so much more than so many other people. He says
more with a scream than so many people do with pages and
pages of words. Take Van Morrison. He makes soul music and some
people have tried to write him off, but he certainly hasn't been.
That man – he's a genius! *November 1984*

**I think a group like us needs a good clip round the ear, a good
kick in the pants, rock'n'roll groups need it. *January 1985***

If you were on the road with us for a long time and if you
saw us in a crisis situation or if you saw things happening around
us... you know what they say, there's two houses built, one's built
on sand, one's built on rock. It's only when a flood comes that you
sometimes see what you've got... there is something we've had
to fight for in the group and it's there.

We all know it's there and it's a real love of each other and
love of what we do and it is a flame, you know and that's the song,
'Indian Summer Sky.' There's times when it feels like it's nearly
been blown out, but it's still there. You might not see it but it's there
and it can ignite into a forest fire or whatever, depending on
what's happening around us. *January 1985*

**The reason we had backed off from the press over the
last three or four years was because we wished to separate
ourselves from a lot of other groups around who were only
too glad to appear on the cover of the teeny-bop press, and as
soon as they had a single out they were in the *Melody Maker*
talking about it. It was a very predictable production-line thing.**

**We pulled away and we knew our fans respected our position
on this, but I see that in some ways it backfired because
it looked as if we were removing ourselves not just from the
business but from our audience. And I think at one point the only
voice being heard was the voice of our critics and the portrayal
of the group was of a cartoon world and we were the characters
in the cartoon. I would look at the person that was supposed
to be me and I didn't recognise this person as being me.**

**The real people that were involved in the group, the Edge,
myself, Larry and Adam, we were lost in all this and that's why,
I suppose, we're rethinking our situation and saying, 'Hold on
a second.' It's a kind of character assessment. *January 1985***

We don't allow people to make jokes in our company.
Anyone on the crew who's ever seen with a smile on their faces
we let go. *May 1985*

**We're the antithesis of those big rock'n'roll bands. This is
not the cycle complete again, this is a garage band that has
left garage-land, because we are the first of that generation of
bands, not The Clash and Sex Pistols generation but the
generation that was in their audience. *June 1985***

What has kept us together? Fear of our manager! *February 1987*

**Musicians have acted like we were taking the piss
when we ask them what a C minor looks like. *March 1987***

Lou Reed recently did an interview where he talked about U2 and said we were at odds with everything that was going on. In our organisation, our road crew, our attitude to money, it was all something different... *March 1987*

In the past, U2 tended never to write songs. We worked within a sound and just manipulated that – improvising and jamming, working with textures and tones and sketching words around them. *March 1987*

Last week when we played some of (Bob) Dylan's songs in Los Angeles I said to him, 'You know, these songs will last forever.' He said, 'Man I think your songs will last forever too – it's just that no-one will be able to play them!' *July 1987*

We can be accused of taking ourselves and our music too seriously. We are the band either naive enough or stupid enough to take rock'n'roll seriously. But we're not trying to start a church. *November 1987*

All over America they had set up these clubs where they listen to U2 records and actually write cards for Amnesty (International). If you can inspire something on that small scale, that's everything I could ask for. All in fact, I would ask for. *November 1987*

When the 'Save The Yuppie' gag came on the news here it was introduced by some guy saying, 'U2, previously concerned with the homeless and the starving etc. etc., now do this.' They went for it. They believed we meant it. We got into terrible trouble. *December 1987*

At home we have an office that takes very seriously any requests for our time or our money. We have our own clear ideas, our own way of redistributing the money we make, and it's between us and the four walls. No-one will ever know. If we were fuzzy about it all, we'd get blown around by every ill will, every lunatic fringe that ever knocked on the door. The worship of money is a strange phenomenon. *December 1987*

We used to believe that everything was possible. Now we believe that some things are possible. *December 1987*

It's not important to be the biggest band in the world. What is important is to be the best. *1987*

People look at U2 and see all these pure motives – but we started off being in a band for the most impure motives. *1988*

It's the old cliché – we want it all and we want it now. The thing about a group is that there's no mountain you won't climb and, of course, one day you're going to end up on the wrong peak wasting your energy. Pete Townshend of The Who told me in the early days that we'd encounter many side roads but that we shouldn't take them. You're in the greatest of things, he said – a real band. *1988*

We intend to make music until people are sick of us. We just don't care at this point. We've nothing to lose. *1988*

Religion

I think the church is a big problem. *February 1981*

It's not all of our beliefs and not everyone in the band believes in the same way. There are things I just don't want to talk about. I'll talk about them in the music, the way I feel about things comes out on-stage. There are things that don't go well coming indirectly from other people. *February 1981*

I don't know much about religion, but I am a Christian.
On their song 'Gloria', 1982

I think people understand now that I'm not religious, they understand that I'm nearly anti-religion...when I talk of religion I'm talking about the force that's cut this country in two. I'm not religious at all, but I believe in God very strongly, and I don't believe that we just kind of exploded out of thin air, I can't believe that. *February 1982*

I think it's the spiritual strength that's essential to the band. People have got to find their own way. I'm not into standing up and saying, 'Hey, you should be into God!' My own life is exhilarating through an experience I feel, and I feel there's no point in talking about something which should be there in your life anyway. You don't have to preach about it. *February 1982*

We used to have this thing – like John Lennon saying of Pete Best, 'He's not a Beatle.' We're all Beatles but we're all radically different people. Three of us are Christians and Adam isn't. That doesn't mean we're going to say to him at any time, you're not in the club. *February 1982*

I have this hunger in me... everywhere I look I see the evidence of a creator. But I don't see it as religion, which has cut Irish people in two. I don't see Jesus Christ as being in any part of a religion. Religion to me is almost like when God leaves – and people devise a set of rules to fill the space. *February 1982*

When Christ was on earth he spent all his time with ordinary people, trying to give them something. I don't see any audience as being full of anti-Christs, you have to look beneath the surface. There are probably more people like that in a church on Sunday. The audience cannot be oblivious to the spiritual side. People just usually sweep it under the carpet, but it's there in their heads. *February 1982*

I'm frightened, but I'm not cynical or pessimistic about the future and a lot of that must come down to my beliefs. It is my belief in God that enables me to get up in the morning and face the world. I believe that there is a logic and a reason for everything. If I didn't believe that and thought that everything was simply down to chance, then I'd really be afraid. I wouldn't cross the road for fear of being run over. *February 1983*

I like to think I'd be as happy in a Catholic church as a Protestant one. *June 1983*

People would love to sensationalise our beliefs until they
meant nothing. Three of us are committed Christians. We refute the
belief that man is just a higher stage of animal, that he has no spirit.
I think that when people start believing that, the real respect for
humanity is gone. You are just a cog in a wheel, another collection
of molecules. That's half the reason for a lot of the pessimism in
the world. *June 1983*

**I have a real sense that I fall short, all the time... I fall short of
being the Christian I want to be.**

Can you imagine how it feels to believe in Christ and be
so uncomfortable with Christianity? The church is an empty, hollow
building. It's the edifice. The established church is the edifice of
Christianity. It's as if when the spirit of God leaves a place, the only
things that are left are the pillars of rules and regulations to keep
its roof on. And we are more and more claustrophobic around
organised religion. I used to think I could walk into a Protestant or
Catholic church or whatever and just be at one with myself and
the surroundings. But we are... it's as if the way we are outsiders in
the music scene we're outsiders on every level. We get flak from
everyone. We seem to be walking this line, and whenever we cross it
either way it's a long way down, on either side, to fall. And I don't
know how we're still there, but it takes it all away to talk about
it too much. *January 1985*

**We don't talk about our personal beliefs because there's too
much talk. You turn on the television (in America) and you have
this guy who looks like a neo-Nazi with a Bible in his hand and
his fist is virtually coming out of the TV screen and into the room
where you're sitting and watching him. The credits come up
and the call for cash comes. Can you imagine how that feels?
For me, it's as much as I can do to restrain myself from throwing
the television out of the top floor of the hotel. It's taught us to
shut up. Let's not be the band that talks about love, let's be
the band that loves its music and the people are attracted to the
music. And even the ones that aren't maybe, as well. But even
that sounds pompous. It's such a claustrophobic position to be
in, being in a group, in some ways. *January 1985***

We don't want to be the band that talks about God. If there's
anything in what we have to say it will be seen in our lives, in our
music and in our performance.
    People have got to find their own way – I'm not standing up and
saying, 'Hey, you should be into God.' *January 1987*

**People expect you, as a believer, to have all the answers,
when really all you get is a whole new set of questions.
There's no question that 'The Unforgettable Fire' took it out
of me and I went through a reappraisal of many things.
I think if 'Still Haven't Found What I'm Looking For' is
successful, it's because it's not affirmative in the ordinary
way of a gospel song. It's restless, and yet there's still a pure
joy in it somewhere. In the relationships between the voice
and Edge's guitar. I guess I'm happy to be unhappy.
*March 1987***

Once we were asked to set up an audience with the Pope. We
were told the Pope wants to meet U2. We thought, 'This is a good
laugh, he must have heard 'Gloria'.' So we got this message and we
said, 'Fair enough, we'll meet anyone.' So I thought, 'Yeah, I'll meet
the Pope, impress the relatives.' In one way I'm attracted to him
because he's Polish and I like Polish people and he has a tender

heart but, on the other hand, he's very conservative and some would say he's put the Catholic church back a few years. So in the end I said, 'Okay, we'll meet him privately.' Word came back from the Vatican, 'No press? No publicity? But ees the whole idea!' I said, 'Sorry, mate, join the queue with the rest of the punters.' *March 1987*

That was great. I really enjoyed it, walking through the Vatican with my stick going, 'One day all of this could be mine!'.
On MacPhisto visiting the Vatican

If a man came up to me and said he was Jesus Christ I'd point him to the bargain basement. It's the 20th century and you can't walk around in those shoes he used to wear. I'd tell him he's in the wrong supermarket. Safeways is better value. On a more serious level I'd say that, if Jesus Christ was on earth you'd probably find him in a gay bar in San Francisco. He'd be working with people suffering from AIDS. These people are the new lepers. Just like the turn of BC/AD. Don't touch them, walk away from them. If you want to find out where Jesus would be hanging out, it'll always be with the lepers. *December 1987*

The new fundamentalists are very, very dangerous. To quote a preacher, 'I had a sneak look at the back of the book' so I know that the good guys will win in the end. In the meantime, the bad guys are in control and religion has become an industry – something that has more in common with McDonalds than it does with me. *December 1987*

I'm a believer, I'm still a believer, but it's the context that people put me in that I resent. *December 1987*

I met this guy once in a mental hospital I was visiting. He introduced himself as Jesus Christ. I just said, 'Haven't we met before?' He said nothing. I asked him why, if he was the son of God, was he in a mental hospital? He said, 'Because it's my 40 days and 40 nights in the wilderness.' At that point I just cracked up. I asked him when the end of the world was going to come. He said April 1. I thought, 'Brilliant, pencil it into the diary. The world will end on April Fool's Day. Perfect.' *December 1987*

All the best songs are co-written by God, y'know! *1987*

The only music I'm interested in is music which is either running towards or away from God.

All our songs are about God or women, and we often get the two mixed up.

I have never been very religious. I don't go in for it myself, I am a believer and that's a very important thing in my life. It's difficult to talk about it because as soon as you do people want to measure you up. I have always thought I am a very bad advert for belief in God and I try to shut up when that subject comes up, which is what I'm going to do. But I feel strongly as I have always felt, I saw something written up on a wall... it said: 'God is dead – Nietzsche' and underneath was 'Nietzsche's dead – God.'

People can think what they like, but there's a sort of art-direction opinion that goes on where it is unacceptable to have belief – and I object to that.

Ireland

The traffic is very fast here in London – the lights go green,
and wham! they move off. In Dublin they'll cough, scratch and then
away they go. It's like Dublin's in a constant state of amber.
November 1979

**Northern Ireland was not affecting me at all. I realised
that. Then it began to affect me. Then I felt sick in the pit of
my stomach about the whole situation. Sick about the fact
that, although 50 miles away from this violence, it was out
of my sight, so it was out of my mind. It didn't bother me.
What did I care?**

**I don't care, I'm not political, I'm not interested in politics,
I despise politics. But it was only from talking to people who
were involved in the situation up north that it's a reality
going on in there. There is war going on in Northern Ireland.
It is war. Whichever side you're on. And I don't want to be
on sides. I don't think there is a solution. It's just part of the
problem of being a human being. We're all violent. But I
was becoming aware of things like that: the fact that I wasn't
aware of that.**

**It's funny that it's been this year, where I've been away
for most of the year that I'm actually starting to think like this.
It's the old situation that when you're taken away from
something that you take for granted you start to think about it.
And I've started to think about it on that level.** *May 1981*

Ireland has a strong tradition of live music. Did you know
the Irish spend more money on live concerts than anywhere
else in the world? This all stems from Irish showbands. These are
groups which travel around the country and play versions of popular
music. When we went round the country we were playing our
own music and people really took notice. It's so hard for kids to go
to gigs. Most music is played at places where you have to be
over 18, sometimes 20.

When we started playing, the whole band was under-age
and so we had open-air gigs. There was Saturday afternoon gigs
in the car park, for example. We'd sweep it out at 10am and there'd
still be clouds of dust when we were on-stage. But it was fantastic;
700 people crammed in and the stage almost collapsed with the
power going on and off. Every time the power went off we'd have
a member of the audience who'd been jeering come up on-stage
and talk to everyone so as to pass the time. It's crazy that there's
nowhere else to play. There are grants for all the other arts but
pop music is never considered important. Yet it's what most young
people are really into. *May 1981*

**The Irish aren't into much bullshit, really. They're not into
designer jeans, you know? They're a more down-to-earth race
and I think they see through the fashion angle pretty quick.
The Irish are also a very aggressive race, which makes for good
rock'n'roll.** *February 1982*

We want to be at home. I don't feel like a Roy Rogers,
a righter of wrongs, but I do feel this personal love for the people
of Dublin. *February 1982*

If you're walking in Dublin you can see 5 or 6 year old kids walk up to policemen and inhale from bags of glue, as if to say, 'Look what I'm doing.' *February 1982*

A lot of people can't handle these times, and they are turning to things like heavy drug abuse. In the area of Dublin where I live there are 15 year old kids using heroin. They can buy little 10 packs for £10. A lot of people just can't handle it. *February 1983*

It was only going to America that made us think of Ireland. You just don't think about it until you have people throwing money on-stage during Bobby Sands and the whole hunger strike thing. I thought that guy must be so brave, but why? Why be so brave? Why die? There's something not right about this. People were going, 'Yeah! You're Irish!' But these people were seeing everything in black and white about Ireland and they didn't realise it was all in the grey. But they know better now, I think, having met people since 'War' I think we contributed to that understanding. *October 1984*

I've said it before, but I didn't know I was Irish until I went to America. It's only recently that I've started to discover the tradition of Irish music. I grew up on groups like The Dubliners, but I turned my back on it. I walked away 'cos I was into rock'n'roll: Ziggy Stardust and The Spiders From Mars, Patti Smith – I had no time for that traditional shit. *1988*

I would like to see a united Ireland, I believe it is an island. People then say do you believe in a cause enough to die for it? I believe in a cause enough to live for it. These people believe in taking other's lives away. I just can't agree with this whole, if you don't agree with me I'll put a gun to your head vibe. Having had a Protestant father and a Catholic mother I know how grey it is. There are no easy sides. *October 1984*

Coming from Ireland you're a bit (aggressive)… so people ask you a question and it's BOP! and it came across as being a little heavy at times. But I never pointed a finger at anybody but myself. Sometimes the tone of my voice gives the impression of a warning, but I never ever point. *November 1984*

I don't know much about politics, but I know a little about people. And I responded to Dr Garrett Fitzgerald, who's now the Prime Minister of the country, as a person more than a politician. See, I met him before he was Prime Minister, in Heathrow Airport. I just walked through the security cordon, pushed them aside, went up and had an argument with him. For about half an hour, y'know. The police were coming up to me, but he said, 'No, no, it's alright.'
**   Then he said, 'Well look, let's continue this conversation when we get to Dublin' so we went on the plane and ended up sitting beside each other and we had another row. It was not in an aggressive way. I was asking him why politicians don't speak the language of the people, why they invented their own language that leaves the rest of the country out. I was saying that any leader of a country had to throw away the political language that they had and speak to the people.**
**   Then he wrote to me and he came down while we were making 'War'. Then, because I'd been mouthing off to him about unemployment he said, 'Well, we're putting together this emergency commission on unemployment – I want you on it.' And I said, 'Well, what can I do?' So essentially, I was the**

trouble-maker. All I could do was arrive at these meetings and when people said, 'What young people feel like', I'd say, 'Hey, I'm one of them.' *November 1984*

I was on the committee to look into the affairs of the unemployed and young people. And I was the only young person on the committee. Garrett Fitzgerald asked me, and I respect the man very much. But they had another language, committee speak, and it wasn't mine. They did some very good work, but I have to say my own contribution wasn't as vital as it could have been. I just felt that if they were going to talk about unmarried mothers, I wanted an unmarried mother to be there and talk.

I wanted to put flesh and blood on to the statistics. It was all part of this personality crisis as to whether making music was really a waste of time, when we should have got on with the real problems. I've come to terms with that. U2 is what I do best. Pete Townshend rapped me on the knuckles and said, 'Leave the social work to old people like me.' *March 1987*

I would love to see a united Ireland, but I never could support a man who put a gun to somebody's head to see that dream come true. *July 1987*

What is Irishness? I don't know. But I know it's not what it was
20 years ago. It's not what's been handed down to us. It's not the
Republican idea that the sons of Mother Ireland should lay down
their lives for their country. These notions have to be rethought.
The idea of the blood sacrifice for Ireland is a dangerous one.
You can see it backfiring in Enniskillen and things like that. It has to
be said that the minority in Northern Ireland were being pushed into
a corner in the Sixties and in '69, when they attempted to rise up
against that sort of oppression, that was when the real embitterment
started and it went wrong for both sides.

**Well we might sit on a fence politically at times... Ireland
seems so politically absurd, that the main parties all have the
same policies... I just look around and see grey.**

It's a funny thing but rock'n'roll bands know an awful lot about
hotels and we spotted one in Dublin which was in danger of closing
down. It was the only place in Dublin which would serve Gavin
Friday when he used to wear dresses in the hay day of punk and we
have a sort of sentimental attachment to it, so we bought it.
It's called The Clarence.

**I'd like to think that U2 has something of the soul
of The Dubliners and something of the spirit of Luke Kelly.
As a singer, he inspired me to sing. I grew up singing his songs
and I'm still singing them because they're worth singing. 1988**

In the Eighties when all kind of success came to us I guess we
were turned into the national football team and people were so on
our side. I guess that when a band gets as big as U2 gets, it can
be a pain in the arse for the people who have to put up with it
all the time, the billboards and 'Aren't they great?' and 'They're great
ambassadors for Ireland' and all. We had so much of that, so the
reaction, naturally, is 'go and fuck off!' I think there's a bit of that
in Ireland.
   But as far as the arts scene goes it's all nicely mixed up
and you'll find Pat McCabe in the same bar as Gavin Friday, as
Joe O'Connor. There's something of a renaissance at the moment,
Dublin is bursting at the seams with ideas and attitudes and it's
not all literature. I'm happy to live there.

**I think we will all need to get back to our roots. In the
Nineties I think people will be listening to traditional Irish music,
or Cajun music, or maybe old soul music... Which is not to say
I want to throw star dust on the past and be a revivalist,
I do want to go forward.**

I do feel like an Irish band. But I've never liked the 'Britpop'
label or 'Irish rock', I think that's all a bit of a mistake. Music is
either good or it's bad, it doesn't really matter what country it comes
from. There is a concerted effort to put everyone in a gang, people
are always trying to make music like football but the charts is the
only similarity. Who's at the top of the league. And as we all know,
the charts are certainly not an indication of playing form. We feel
strongly Irish, but what it is that makes us Irish is not the obvious,
it's not the tin whistles and pipes. There's something more, it's a
new kind of Irishness. I don't like the old kind of Irish, I never really
felt a part of it.

Songwriting

I rang Edge the other night and told him I'd discovered this thing called The Song. U2 never wrote songs as such. We used to structure pieces of music, working in terms of atmosphere, texture and tones. So I said, 'Look, there's this great thing called Songs. You write them and they go on the radio and they're played all over the world and people listen to them in traffic jams and going to work and The Song becomes part of their day. It's a really far out thing, The Song.' *May 1985*

I called the Edge to tell him all this and he said, 'Oh yeah, I think I know what you mean – wasn't 'Pride' one of those?' And I realised we'd already written some songs! And something I've realised is that for me as a singer, I've got to stop trying to explain myself and to start writing songs that explain myself. June 1985

I often use words not for what they mean but for what they sound like, the way they bump up against other words or things like that. I'm more interested in impression than detail at the moment. I'd like to start using everyday speech – as I'm getting more and more interested in the folk tradition. As they said of Brendan Behan, if the English hoard words the Irish spend them. They just throw words and see what happens. I think as I go on I am going to work towards a balance between the impression and the detail. *November 1984*

The Irish poets gave me a sense for language and for the sound of language, the sense that's in the word, in the sound of the words, things like that.

In the past U2 never tended to write songs. We worked within a sound and just manipulated that. I used to think of lyrics as being old fashioned, with the result that U2 would produce pieces of music rather than songs... Larry, who is probably the most song-orientated member of U2, nudged us in that direction. We'd just come back from an extremely long and exhausting tour and all the routine involved in that. Larry wanted to just get the guys together in his room and simply play music. So we started writing songs. We sat down and wrote these chords and the words. After all these years we decided to come clean. *March 1987*

I used to write words separate from U2. I believed that rock'n'roll wasn't the place for words. So I was just a sketch artist with U2 – I'd try to paint a picture really quickly: just throw a bit of paint on and let it dribble down the edges. 1988

I didn't really begin spending a lot of time on lyrics until halfway into the Eighties. *September 1993*

Irish poets Seamus Heaney and Patrick Kavanagh were a great influence on my writing. Ali's mother and father grew up in Irishtown, which is right in the centre of Dublin, and they remember Kavanagh walking the canal in his great, dirty raincoat. 1988

The only concessions we make are for ourselves. We play the
music that inspires us and, within the last two or three years,
we've discovered a whole world of music: folk, country, blues,
gospel – and occasionally, we will try to reinterpret a song like Curtis
Mayfield's 'People Get Ready.' But we're actually very bad at playing
other people's songs and that's the reason we started to write
our own. *1988*

**Whenever people talk about our music having messages,
it makes me feel like a postman. As the writer of the words,
I write about things the way that I see them. I never set out
to change the world, just to change my own world. Rock'n'roll
is a noise that has woken me up and it's good that, if along
the way, it wakes other people up. I do feel we mustn't fall
asleep in the comfort of our freedom. Also Edge can say more
about the struggle in El Salvador with his guitar than I can
with words. *1988***

I don't know if any one song is the best song ever written.
I find it very hard to even listen to our songs because I have no real
objectivity but I find the ones I like most are usually the ones that
came the easiest.

**I can't listen to anything from the early Eighties because
I sound like a girl and that offends my machismo... We didn't
really know what rock'n'roll was back then and I think that's
one of the reasons why we were special. But coming over here
was extraordinary for us, we were completely, in one sense,
out of touch with the mood of the Eighties.
     The groups that people were excited about were cool
whereas we were hot and passionate, operatic or whatever it
was. Rather than being gothic we went more ecstatic and I
had a haircut that launched a million Second Division soccer
players and... well, one in the First Division. But we really didn't
know what we were doing and we were coming from such a
completely different planet. When I listen back, I can see what
was good about them, but I see an awful lot of unfinished songs,
songs I wished I had finished. But the band sounded great.**

A lie is fabricated by a tabloid, and repeated as fact by a
credible paper. At first you feel offended when this happens,
you feel violated, reduced. But after a while you realise that there's
a persona being created and really you are only collaborating.
It's more interactive than you had first imagined, they stick bits
on you, they make you longer or shorter, wider or more interesting
than you in fact are... meanwhile you stop looking for the truth
to be told anywhere other than in the performance of the songs.
You start living in the songs.

The Albums

Boy

'Stories For Boys'... I can remember as a child looking into the mirror and thinking, 'I don't look like that.' It's wrong. It's forced on you all the time, by television. Strength, power – nobody's like that, but you're bombarded with all these images. The effect is total disillusionment with yourself, so you put on a mask and hide from yourself, from your own soul, what you've got to offer. *June 1980*

When our first album came out a guy in the Village Voice wrote about all the fifths and ninths in our music and the most obscure chords and keys. He didn't realise we tuned down to E Flat for my voice. *March 1987*

October

I listened to it last week for the first time in ages and I couldn't believe I was part of it. It's a huge record, I couldn't cope with it. I remember the pressures it was made under, I remember writing lyrics on the microphone and at £50 an hour that's quite a pressure. Lillywhite was pacing up and down the studio... he coped really well. And the ironic thing about 'October' is that there's a kind of peace about the album even though it was recorded under that pressure. *February 1982*

A lot of people found 'October' hard to accept at first. I mean, I used the word 'Rejoice' precisely because I knew people have a mental block against it. It's a powerful word. It's implying more than 'get up and dance, baby.' *February 1982*

Every second of every hour is to be enjoyed. There's a passage in Jeremiah 29 – 'And you will seek me and find me when you shall search for me with all your heart.' There is a very cold atmosphere in the world at the moment. We called our record 'October' to reflect that, but also to suggest a revaluation. I do believe that there is a purpose to everybody's lives, if they yield to that purpose. *February 1982*

I think that 'October' goes into areas that most rock'n'roll bands ignore. *February 1982*

I like it more than I did at first. It's like '11 O'Clock Tick Tock' – that didn't get a great reaction when it was released, but it came through two years or a year later. *January 1983*

War

'New Year's Day' is a love song that is more potent for being set against a background of oppression. Subconsciously I must have been thinking about Lech Walesa being interned and his wife not being allowed to see him. Then when we

released the song they announced that martial law would be lifted in Poland on New Year's Day. *January 1983*

'War' is important to me, the whole band. But make or break? I don't think so, more of a progressive build-up. We have developed the sound, taking it a stage further. It is far more rhythmic, with much more depth. 'War' is our heaviest album yet, it hits you right there. This band is having a go at all the blippety bop aural wallpaper we have rammed down our throats on the radio and the TV everyday. I am personally bloody sick of every time I switch on the radio of being blasted with this contrived crap. *January 1983*

It would be stupid to start drawing up battle lines, but I think that the fact 'New Year's Day' made the Top 10 indicated a disillusionment among record buyers with the pop stuff in the chart. I don't think 'New Year's Day' was a pop single, certainly not in the way Mickie Most might define a pop single as something that lasts three minutes and three weeks in the chart. I don't think we could have written that kind of a song.

People are growing disillusioned with pop, with the wallpaper music and the gloss. It's as if someone has eaten too many Smarties over the last couple of years, and suddenly they're beginning to feel ill as they look at all the wrapping paper strewn around the room. *February 1983*

When we were making 'War' we went practically to the brink of breaking up the band. When we go into the studio we draw totally on our deepest resources and stretch them to the limit. If a band is going to be honest they've got to bring out everything, even the things that might frighten them. *February 1983*

'War' is not a negative LP. I mean, I'm in love and there is a lot of love in the album. A song like 'New Year's Day' might be about war and struggle, but it is also about love. It is about having faith to break through and survive against all the odds. Love is a very powerful thing. There's nothing more radical than two people loving each other.

I think that love stands out when set against a struggle. That's probably the power of the record in a nutshell. The album is about the struggle for love, not about war in the negative sense. I would be failing if I made 'War' sound like a gloomy album because it's not. I hope it's an uplifting record.

Some love songs devalue the meaning of the word. Disco bands turn it into a cliché by tearing it down until it means nothing. The power of love is always more striking when set against realism than when set against escapism. *February 1983*

War seemed to be the motif for 1982. Everywhere you looked, from the Falklands to the Middle East to South Africa, there was war. *February 1983*

A lot of the songs on 'October' were quite abstract, but 'War' is intentionally more direct, more specific. But you can still take the title on a lot of different levels. We're not only interested in the physical idea of war (we're interested in the idea) on an emotional level. *February 1983*

People have become numb to violence. Watching the television it's hard to tell the difference between fact and fiction. One moment you see someone being shot on *The Professionals*, and the next you see someone falling through a window after being shot on the

news. One is fiction and one is real life, but we're becoming so used
to the fiction that we become numb to the real thing. That's one
of the ways in which we're dealing with the subject on the LP.
'War' could be the story of a broken home, a family at war. Instead
of putting tanks and guns on the cover we've put a child's face.
'War' can also be a mental thing, an emotional thing between lovers.
It doesn't have to be a physical thing. There is such a thing
as mental war. We're fascinated by all the different aspects and
connotations. *February 1983*

**I believe that more than any other record 'War' is right for its
time. It is a slap in the face against the snap, crackle and pop.
Everyone else is getting more and more style-orientated,
more and more slick. John Lennon was right about that kind
of music; he called it 'wallpaper music.' Very pretty, very well
designed, music to eat your breakfast to. Music can be more.
Its possibilities are great. Music has changed me. It has
the ability to change a generation. Look at what happened
with Vietnam. Music changed a whole generation's attitude
towards war. *June 1983***

With 'Boy' and 'October' I got flak because they were so abstract.
So with 'War' I decided to strip it right down. I listened to it for
the first time the other day and there were some great songs there.
Though for the first time I could see a strident quality that was
letting me down. I could see how it might have sounded like a finger
pointing, and of course we've never pointed a finger at anyone,
apart from ourselves. That voice was very angry. I didn't realise I
was so tense. *October 1984*

**It was really difficult, that period after 'War'. It was awful.
I was a madman. You know what they do to terrorists in
Northern Ireland? They put brown paper bags over their heads,
they put them in rooms where they can't stand up or sit down
with their legs stretched out, they keep the light on 24 hours a
day so they don't know what time it is or whether it's night
or day.**

    **When you become a piece of luggage, when you're on the
road, you can sometimes lose track of yourself. Completely and
utterly. You become lost in time and space. You walk out on
to a stage, you give of yourself for an hour and a half, and the
applause that comes back is uplifting, but sometimes it's
anonymous. You leave the venue and I need to talk to people
afterwards, I need for that applause to be personified in some
way so I can get a grip on what's been going on. But if you don't,
you end up going back into this empty space which is your
hotel room... a bit like the guy with the paper bag over his head.**
January 1985

'War'... was a reaction to the new romantic movement,
the cocktail set mentality... and deliberately we stripped our sound
to bare bones and knuckles and three capital letters, WAR, and
we put these prime colours in. But we've stood accused since then
for that one album. You could say the same thing about John
Lennon. He went through a similar sort of period, or Bob Dylan on
his earlier work – 'Masters Of War' and all that. It was just a period
he went through. *March 1987*

**Around the time of 'October' and 'War' we weren't even sure
if we wanted to be in a band. I thought rock'n'roll was really just
pure vanity and there didn't seem to be a place in it for some
of the spiritual concerns in my writing. I felt like a fish out of
water, the square peg in the round hole. But I've since realised
that a lot of the artists who have inspired me – Bob Dylan,
Van Morrison, Patti Smith, Al Green, Marvin Gaye – were in a
similar position. They all had three sides to their writing –
sexual, the spiritual and the political. In our own way U2 have
that same three-dimensional thing. That's why I'm more at ease.**
March 1987

During this period I was influenced by the John Lennon
handbook. I had it in my breast pocket. 'Sunday Bloody Sunday'...
after all, John Lennon wrote the first one. What upsets me is that
when people see U2 they see only 'Sunday Bloody Sunday' and the
guy with the white flag. They don't see 'Drowning Man' which was
on the same album. There is another side to U2. Sure we arrived
with a placard in our hands – and bold placards – but that's not just
what U2's about. *March 1987*

**'War' was deliberately bare... in order to set ourselves against
what was going on at the time, the all-dressed-up-and-nowhere-
to-go syndrome, the hiding behind the haircuts. It just so
happens that we came to popularity with 'War', so we're
associated with that. *March 1987***

It wasn't so much the IRA as Republican people took heart
from it because there had been a massacre and it wasn't forgotten
about and was within a song. I guess the only thing I objected to
was that people missed the whole point of the song. I was trying
to contrast – and imagine trying to pull this one off – Easter Sunday
and Bloody Sunday.

    A lot of those lyrics I'm very proud of, and I'm proud of
them almost because they were written so quickly and so naively...

That song was almost entirely written very, very quickly. But it's a big idea to take on. And, oh I don't know anymore… I've had enough bruises and scars not to want to take things head on in the same way anymore. I think you've got to be smarter now.
On 'Sunday Bloody Sunday'.

We broke up the band after 'War'. We literally broke up the band and formed another band with the same name and the same members. That's what we did. We had all those teething problems that you have when you start a new band.
January 1985

Under A Blood Red Sky

I think I lost myself at various points and became an utter madman. That US festival thing. I climbed to the very top of the stage, it was like hundreds of feet up, and walked across the top of it on the canvas, and the canvas ripped. God! I can't watch that! I don't know who that person is. I don't know who it is, climbing up there. I'm afraid of heights, anyway. *January 1985*

'Under A Blood Red Sky' was the logical extension of 'War'. It was a fiery performance because that's how we felt. We were flying in the face of the whole synthipop thing. At the end we'd got it completely out of our systems, but the image didn't leave us behind. *March 1987*

The Unforgettable Fire

That is a record totally devoid of the tracks and techniques of rock'n'roll – which is why it's foxing half the USA even as we speak. *October 1984*

People talk about the spirituality of U2 and I realised that was part of everyday life in black music. Indeed, Jimi Hendrix was the wildest rock'n'roll performer; and Janis Joplin would've loved to be black. I realised though we weren't rooted in black music there was something in the spirit that was similar. *October 1984*

'Elvis Presley In America' was recorded in five minutes. Eno (Brian Eno, producer) just handed me a microphone and told me to sing over this piece of music that had been slowed down, played backwards or whatever. I said, 'What, just like that? Now?' He said, 'Yes, this is what you're all about.' So I did it and when it was finished there were all these beautiful lines and melodies coming out of it. I said, 'I can't wait to finish this.' He said, 'What do you mean finish it? It is finished!' *October 1984*

All Brian had listened to for three years was gospel music. It was the spirit in which it was made that attracted him to the group's music, the sense of abandonment. *October 1984*

With Eno we rediscovered the spirit of our music and a confidence in ourselves. The emphasis was on the moment in this recording, on the spontaneity. It's like that Irish tradition, the Joyce thing, when you're relaxed you're not inhibited. The recording atmosphere was very relaxed. *October 1984*

When Eno came to us for 'The Unforgettable Fire' he talked about rock'n'roll with a wink, how rock'n'roll had become a parody of itself... and how it was only acceptable with a wink. It's white music that is the problem, it's white music that is the strait-jacket. White people in their suits and ties – and under their torn shirts they're still wearing them – are afraid to take off their trousers in public. And somebody's got to burst the bubble, not for us because we've burst it ourselves and we've kind of set ourselves free, but for all the people who aren't making the music they could be making because... because somebody winked and their eyes got stuck.

There's a spell that's gonna have to be broken, in London, in New York, in the music business. I don't know how it's gonna be broken but I just sense that a lot of people are crippled emotionally, withered... I think there's a lot of music that so wants to be made, and it's so frightened and scared. *June 1985*

'The Unforgettable Fire' was a beautifully out-of-focus record, blurred like an impressionist painting, very unlike a billboard or an advertising slogan. These days we are being fed a very air-brushed, advertising-man's way of seeing the world. In the cinema I find myself reacting against the perfect cinematography and the beautiful art direction – it's all too beautiful, too much like an ad. *October 1987*

There's always been two sides to U2, the energy and the atmosphere. With Steve Lillywhite it was always the energy that was showing, but now Brian Eno is helping bring out the atmosphere again. *November 1984*

'Pride' is the best song we've ever written. We've done very few songs... normally we just make music. 'I Will Follow' was a song, but then the next one wasn't until 'Sunday Bloody Sunday.' It's very different from the rest of the album though – there's nothing on there as straight as this. *November 1984*

Last year this band got a little bit lost and this song represents a return to our initial aims, as does the whole of 'The Unforgettable Fire'. Really we've got nowhere near our goals yet. *November 1984*

'Wire' for me is an image of a hypodermic needle. That's its subconscious value to me. I'm intrigued that often imagery that is for me subconscious is actually quite conscious to other people. A guy, somebody in the music business in London, came up to me in the Portobello Hotel and told me he had nearly died last year. Three cardiac arrests, three overdoses. He got involved in Narcotics Anonymous and sorting his life out.

He told me that our music was a real soundtrack to a change in his life. And – this completely bowled me over – he knew everything I was on about on 'The Unforgettable Fire'. He knew what 'Bad' was about, he knew all the feelings, he knew what 'Wire' was about. He knew the two songs that were related directly to what he'd been through. As abstract as they were. *May 1985*

I was at a demonstration at Columbia University the other week. It was a hunger strike against what's happening in South Africa. I went down there and found that 'Pride' was on their tape; they were listening to it in their sleeping bags in the pissing rain and that gave me some encouragement. That's not why you set out to write a song – but if it has an impact on another person's life as much as it's had on your life, well, I'm pleased. I'm also very pleased because a lot of our fans

have been getting involved in things like famine relief organisations and anti-nuclear movements. People just feeling, 'Yeah, I'm going to find my place in this.' That's their place, off-stage. *May 1985*

In America when we put out 'The Unforgettable Fire' there was such a backlash. People thought we were the future of rock'n'roll and they went, 'What are you doin' with this doggone hippie Eno album?' We owe Eno and Lanois so much for seeing through to the heart of U2. *March 1987*

The Joshua Tree

Smart people put on 'The Joshua Tree' and think to themselves, 'I'm gonna play this a lot of times.' Foolish people would put it on and just go, 'WOW! YEAH!' and think they've got a line on it. I think this record, more than any of the others, says what we want to say. Certainly for me, as the word writer in the band. In a way it doesn't need me to do the interviews to explain it. After a while it does sink in, the way it's put together from beginning to end. The significance of the name 'The Joshua Tree' – it's almost impossible for me to explain that seriously, for me to take myself as seriously as that. There are many reasons for it. Inevitably, we're gonna have to lie a lot. *March 1987*

In the song 'With Or Without You' when it says 'and you give yourself away' – everybody else in the group knows what that means. It's about how I feel in U2 at times – exposed.

I used to think writing words was old-fashioned, so I sketched. I wrote words on the microphone. For 'The Joshua Tree' I felt the time had come to write words that meant something, out of my experience. *March 1987*

On this record I'm interested in a lot of primitive symbolism, almost Biblical. Some people choose to use red, some people choose turquoise. Some people like lavender. I like red. *March 1987*

'Joshua Tree'... it's a very odd town on the edge of the California desert. A lot of the psychedelic writers came out of there. Gram Parsons was buried there. It's the sort of record title you'd expect to sell three copies of. *March 1987*

Greg Carroll (to whom the LP is dedicated) was almost flesh and blood with U2. We met him in Auckland, New Zealand... and he worked with us on 'The Unforgettable Fire' Tour... he was one of those guys you say is too good for this world. We haven't, and I don't think we ever will, get over his loss. And he died doing me a favour. I don't know what to say. He further made 1986 the most paradoxical year in our lives. That's why the desert attracted me as an image. That year was really a desert for us, it was a terrible time. Death is a real cold shower and I've had a lot. It's followed me around since I was a kid and I don't want to see any more of it. *March 1987*

I wrote 'Bullet The Blue Sky' out of fear while I was there (El Salvador), using very primitive imagery. Because Salvador looks like an ordinary city. You see McDonalds, you see children with school books, you see what looks like a middle-class

environment until you go 25 miles out of the city and see the villagers and peasant farmers dead on the side of the road… or disappeared. *March 1987*

A lot of the songs were ones that were recorded in Larry's spare bedroom or Adam's living room. When the red light's on we often don't respond to it. When we're just left to be, left to make music our own way, well some of the tracks are almost like demos. We had to fight to make them work and there were a lot of songs left over. It could have gone off in a number of different directions. We wanted the idea of a one-piece record, not a side-one, side-two thing. *March 1987*

The lack of inhibition of the Seventies, though it can go wrong, is right to a point. In the Eighties, people are so claustrophobic and won't make mistakes and a lot of these young bands see themselves as part of the Seventies rock'n'roll tradition. They want to get away from this feeling of we-can't-play-guitar-like-that. The answer is, you can do what you like. That's what 'Joshua Tree' is about. There's electric blues wound up in 'Bullet The Blue Sky', or a simple piano piece. We were feeling bound up as well, in U2, with this sound we'd developed. We didn't want to go down in the A-Z of rock'n'roll as a band without a sound. We wanted to leave some songs. *March 1987*

'With Or Without You', it's a great single… God almighty, I hope it gets into the Top 10, I really do. It's a classic 45. *March 1987*

Scott Walker's 'Climate Of Hunter', that was a great influence on our LP. Listen to 'With Or Without You'… *March 1987*

Record company executives… they say the major rock'n'roll album

from this major rock'n'roll band, what's it called? 'The Joshua Tree'? It's almost worth it to see their faces! *March 1987*

The spirit in which we recorded it was akin to the idea of a gospel group. We wanted to capture a moment, the feeling of a room and people being in a room, which is essential to gospel music. Eno was a real ally in this. He listens to more gospel music than anything else. *March 1987*

I was so scared that the record has been so BIG and we would enter Kevin and Sharon territory – that we'd attract an audience that is just into big bands like the Stones and Queen and aren't really a partisan audience. Even at Wembley we found this just wasn't the case. We found out there was still a U2 audience, people who had been to the first gigs, people that had bought 'Boy', people who were growing with us, changing with us. I only hope they will be with us next year. *December 1987*

When I was reading about the Miners' Strike, what particularly interested me aside from the politics – because you can get bogged down in that – was the breaking down of relationships and what the strike had done to people's sex lives. Literally, y'know, men and women couldn't relate to each other through losing work and losing belief in themselves. And I wrote the words to 'Red Hill' about a year after the strike. *1988*

During and since 'The Joshua Tree' myself and Edge would be up at six o'clock in the morning then Adam'd drop in just writing songs and playing records. We haven't stopped writing songs: they just keep coming and coming and coming. *1988*

'Silver And Gold' is the first song that I've ever written from somebody else's point of view. U2 songs are always from my point of view, but this is a departure into the third person. It's also the first blues-influenced song I've written, I play the guitar with my foot miked up, the way that old bluesmen like Robert Johnson used to do. And I'm banging the sides of my guitar with my knuckles to keep the rhythm. As the song goes on the tempo keeps getting faster and the mood more and more intense. *January 1986*

The line that started it for me was one about a boxer, the idea of a prize fighter in his corner being egged on by a trainer. It's a sport that I've found increasingly interesting over the past year. I find a lot of aspects of it very sordid, a bit like cock fighting, or something, but the image was very powerful for the song.
On 'Silver and Gold' January 1986

We, as a group, formed our sound devoid of any background because our record collections started in 1976 with Tom Verlaine, Patti Smith and The Clash and the Jam. 'Silver And Gold' was my desperate attempt – and I wrote it in two hours – to write a song that belonged to a tradition. I was writing it about South Africa, about a man who was at the point of violence, which is something that fascinates me. *March 1987*

Rattle And Hum – The Record

I wanted to get away from the sort of imagery that was on 'The Unforgettable Fire'. For years I had been writing all these words which I could never use for U2. I could never fit them into songs.

They were words with harder edges. I was in a sense looking for a new U2 where I could feel free to use these words.

I also felt left out of the rock'n'roll tradition, like when T-Bone Burnett played me a song and then handed me the guitar and asked me to play one of mine. In that sense U2 is more like an orchestra than a rock'n'roll band. You can't just sit down and strum 'The Unforgettable Fire' or 'Bad'... As far as I remember I turned the guitar over and just beat the back and sang a song or two. This feeling of wanting to be able to write songs in the traditional sense led to songs like 'Silver And Gold.'

I'm dependent on music in a way. In writing words and music I'm attempting to identify myself. We're all trying to find out who we are and music is like that for me. I find that I almost hold on to it in a very desperate way. I want to reveal the dark side as well as the light side of who I am. *October 1988*

'Desire' is about ambition... the ambition to be in a band. You don't join a band to save the world but to save your own arse and get off the street. You want to play to the crowd rather than be in the crowd. I wanted to own up to all this because people look at U2 and see all these pure motives – but we started off being in a band for the most impure motives. We started off through just being bored at school. We didn't want to get a job in a factory or work for the government. We didn't want to be school teachers or join the army or whatever. People get in bands for all the wrong reasons, not the right reasons. *October 1988*

I woke up with an awful bleedin' hangover, one day, and I had a melody in my head. Some of the words were in my head at the same time and I thought 'Oh God, do I have to write this down now?' I just wanted to go back to bed. But I couldn't avoid it, so I wrote it down. The start of this song sounded like a Bob Dylan song. I thought maybe it was a Bob Dylan song – signs of megalomania in that too. So I happened to be seeing him later on that day and I went up and said, 'This isn't one of yours is it?' And he said, 'No, but you know, we could write it now.' So we wrote it. *On 'Love Rescue Me.'*

What other band in our position would learn the chords of 'All Along The Watchtower' five minutes before they went on-stage, play it live and record it? No one. *October 1988*

Basically instead of putting out a double live LP we chose to put out 'Rattle And Hum'. The double live LP has been exciting over the years, but with very few exceptions it's a pile of crap and basically a cash-in by big fat rock bands like U2 to extort more money from their fans. We felt that if we were going to put out a soundtrack to a film we'd better put out something more interesting... so we came up with 'Rattle And Hum'... it's just our way round the problem. *November 1988*

We visited the Sun Studios (where some of 'Rattle And Hum' was recorded). It was amazing... We had Cowboy Jack Clemmons in on the session. He's the guy who recorded Jerry Lee Lewis' 'Whole Lotta Shakin.' I found this old microphone with cobwebs on it and said, 'Cowboy Jack, will you look at this. It looks like something Elvis would have sung into.' I found that he really did sing into it.

After 10 minutes, this mike that had recorded 'Mystery Train' and a load of other classics was working again. Then he told me where Elvis used to stand, but I thought he was taking things a little too far. *December 1987*

Sun Studios is a remarkable place. I mean, really, there are all these photographs of Elvis Presley, Jerry Lee Lewis, Johnny Cash… this is the room where rock'n'roll was born! And it was a totally mindblowing privilege to be playing there. In fact I'm embarrassed to say this, but I saw this old microphone in the corner and I asked the producer if I could use it, and he said, 'Elvis used this mike but it doesn't work now.' So I said, 'Are you sure?' so he plugged it in and it worked! It really did work! And actually – this sounds like total bullshit, but it's the truth – 'Angel Of Harlem' was recorded singing through Elvis' mike! I only wish I could sing like Elvis. *November 1988*

We wrote 'Desire' in five minutes, we recorded it in five minutes and it's true, it's a demo we put out. We nearly chickened out of it but we didn't. *November 1988*

I think a lot of people who don't like the record, and a lot of people who don't like U2, actually haven't listened to U2. It tends to be that they hear a record on the radio or someplace else. *1989*

('Hawkmoon')'s my favourite, the last few seconds of that scare the shit out of me. And 'God Part II', the Edge's guitar. *1989*

Our audience has proved to be an elastic kind of audience. They're into the where-to-next kind of approach. They're one step ahead of us in some ways. Rather than to have to lead the audience around by the nose we get the sense that they're right behind us every step of the way. We thought if we stripped away the U2 sound completely, if we immersed ourselves in gospel music, country, soul… we're bound to shake off at least 50 per cent of U2 fans: they can't cope with this. But they really could. We might have the most elastic audience when you think of what we've gone through in the last five years. As long as the songs are good they'll go with us all the way. When we start writing shit songs then I'll know it's over. *1989*

Rock'n'roll is a great tradition and we are part of it – and maybe you'll think this is funny – but we thought it was, kind of, the most humble thing to do. This was a record made by fans – we wanted to own up to being fans. And we thought rock'n'roll bands just didn't do that – we all know they are, but they don't do it. The Rolling Stones did it on 'Exile On Main Street', sort of, and it was kind of a role model. But we wanted to go even further and have pictures because there's people out there who probably don't even know who Billie Holiday is or who BB King is. We thought it was, 'We have this thing, U2; now let's just put it aside almost and let's just get lost in this music.' *November 1991*

If people didn't like 'Rattle And Hum' they won't like what's coming. I don't mean that in musical terms – I mean that we're going to continue to put out records in that kind of way. We've started to make records now for ourselves and for our own audience who do listen very carefully to all our records and who do spot all the subtleties. We're the Grateful Dead of the Nineties. *November 1991*

I mean the thing about Spinal Tap sort of, is that it's all true. I mean, you know we went to Gracelands, and we stared down Spinal Tap. I mean, we went to Gracelands and we – well, at least we did laugh, but we edited those bits out… Now, we smirk. *March 1992*

Maybe we just weren't paying attention. The whole thing
was just throwaway to us, in the best sense of the word – not just
the movie, but the record. That showed us just how powerful the
media is. We genuinely believed it was a record about being fans of
rock'n'roll. And we put a bit of Johnny Cash there and a song
about Billie Holiday here to kind of show we were just fans. It was
so obvious to us. Maybe we didn't understand how successful we
were and that it looked like we were hanging out with these guys so,
by association, that we were one of the greats. We never saw it
that way. *February 1993*

Rattle And Hum – The Film

**I thought I looked like Robert Wagner until I saw myself on
screen. I ended up watching this thing on-stage. The idea for
the film was that the Director, Phil Joanou, would make us all
look like movie stars. The deal was that we'd all look like
Montgomery Clift.** *October 1988*

We needed someone robust enough to stand life on the road,
the whole lifestyle. Phil (Joanou, director) had to be capable of
being locked up in a flight case.
    We responded to him in the end and he prised the best
possible film out of us. One thing I didn't like about Phil Joanou
though – he was better looking than me. *November 1988*

**I wish ('Sunday Bloody Sunday') wasn't in the film in one
sense. In another sense I stand by everything I said because it
was the truth. It was the way we felt, on that day, on that night.
It's more of a tribute to Phil Joanou than it is to me 'cos he
talked us into it and, personally, I'm not sure that we'll ever play
that song again. That's the way I feel about it. I've just about had
it up to here with 'Sunday Bloody Sunday' as a song and the
weight it carries.** *November 1988*

Achtung Baby

There have been false accusations of us hyping our record
which is the last thing we need to do. That is why we are keeping
quiet, we are not doing interviews, we are not talking to anybody
and we just want the music to speak for itself. You can't make
somebody buy a record.
    I just can't believe that we've finished the record and that it's out.
That's what's amazing to me, because we've been working on it for
about a year and you forget that when it's out people are going to be
listening to it in the kind of way they are. It's been really amazing to
hear people singing the songs and getting lost in the music. I really
love that, it's great. *November 1991*

**I certainly think this record, 'Achtung Baby' is a new start,
and things move in shifts. I mean, there's another record that
belongs with this, just as 'Rattle And Hum' belonged with
'The Joshua Tree'. I know that record, I can hear it in my head.
And we have notes, we have songs already for our next record
as it happens. There's more where that came from. So I can see
further down the road.** *February 1992*

It's a con! It's a con. It's just a way of putting people off
from the fact that it's a heavy mother. It's probably our most serious
record – and yet it's got the least serious title. And it just fooled
everyone. They all thought we were, you know, we'd lightened up.
Which is totally untrue. We're miserable bastards. *March 1992*

**The album wasn't an easy ride for listeners, when they first
bought it. But, isn't that what rock'n'roll should be right now,
is a bit awkward, a bit hard to digest? I mean, we live in
this junk food generation, where everything is so nice, and it's
air brushed – and you, you know, it's easily digested – and the
way I look at it, it's just as easy to spit it out. And I think
that rock'n'roll shouldn't be so easily explained – it should take
a while. You know, it shouldn't be on a plate. *March 1992***

Yeah, it's a song about hypocrisy. It's a song about my
own hypocrisy as much as anything. That's what we started on
'Achtung Baby'. It was just to get into the politics of your own heart
and start with that. *On 'Acrobat'*

**We thought everyone was just sick and tired of hearing us talk,
so we decided that we wouldn't... not until we figured out what
we wanted to say.**
    **We just didn't want to do interviews, basically, because it
was the predictable thing to do, and also what happens is you
finish an album, and immediately after you've got to go off
and start explaining yourself – and that's just the wrong moment
to do that, because you're so wrapped up in it. *April 1992***

The thing about bootlegs is... the only thing that can piss you
off is if people are charging a lot of money for something that isn't
very good, and that was maybe the story on ('Achtung Baby').
It got bootlegged from Berlin and it was just like having your
notebook read out. That's the bit I didn't like about it... There were
no great undiscovered works of genius, unfortunately, it was mostly
gobbledygook... but there were a few bits and pieces on that
bootleg that I actually liked, when I got a copy of the bootleg...
I had to go out and buy one, of course, myself. *April 1992*

**Oh, there's lots of stories in there, by no means only his.
In fact, it's the story of just about everybody I know. People are
desperately trying to hold on to each other in a time when it's
very hard to do that. And the bittersweet love song is something
I think we do very well. It's a tradition, and Roy Orbison was
probably the greatest in that tradition. *On Edge's divorce being
the inspiration for some of 'Achtung Baby', February 1993***

There's a station in Berlin... Zoo Bahnhof, which was the link
between the East and the West. And it was where all the immigrants
came through on their shopping sprees into West Berlin. It was
also where a lot of hookers hung out and a lot of deals were done.
And it just so happened that one of the lines running into the
tube-station part of it was the U2 line and we couldn't resist
the chance to follow that line... *On Hansa Studios, February 1992*

**The Hansa Studio, where we recorded 'Achtung Baby', was
used both by the Allies and the SS as a ballroom. And when we
went in there we asked ourselves, 'Are there still any demons
in the room?' We had the sense that if there had been any
demons, music had driven them out. I think fear of the devil
leads to devil worship. And I don't want to give fascists the**

power over you to the extent you might be afraid to go into a building where they once were. You should take these icons and change them. *August 1993*

I started writing the songs that became 'Achtung Baby' (in Sydney, Australia). There was a woman living (in the apartment opposite) I used to watch when I'd come in at six, seven in the morning. She was overweight, had a punk haircut, and used to get home around the same time I did. I made up a whole life for her – that she ran a punk club, that her parents financed it for her. I started watching her through a telescope. We excuse a lot in the name of reconnaissance! One night I was watching her and I happened to look two windows above her. There was another woman with another telescope watching me! I was furious! I was so offended, I jumped up and called her a bitch and pulled the curtains shut. *May 1995*

Zooropa

I know how it feels to have that emotional charge coming at you night after night while U2 are touring, and there is a process that can best be described as coming down after a tour. There are DTs involved, but it's not alcohol or drugs as such that you're addicted to. There is no name for the substance, but it certainly exerts a hold over your life after a tour ends.
    The new album, in a way it was an attempt to tune into that energy and stay up during the break in the tour rather than come down to earth again. This time we said, 'Okay we're up on the moon so let's stay here and make a record.' But that was our choice, to coast on that feeling rather than risk falling. So in essence, the album could be seen as a substitute 'hit' for us, between tours. But it remains to be seen whether it will be as much of a 'hit' with everyone else! But I am also conscious that there is a part of me that doesn't want to come home. Part of me wants to stay on the moon. But as to whether I am addicted to that feeling, I honestly don't know. I can't give you the answer to that. *August 1993*

That's what I want it to be! Legal drugs. Why else would you buy an album these days? Have you read anything by (William) Gibson? It's sort of fucked-up sci-fi. And ('Zooropa') shows you what I mean when I say the textures on this record were very much influenced by what he writes about the future. *August 1993*

This is called 'Babyface.' And in this brightly-lit, fucked up commercial landscape we'll have on-stage, we take the audience through a window and there's a guy watching somebody on a TV, a personality, a celebrity he's obsessed with. It's about how people play with images, believing you know somebody through an image and think that by manipulating a machine that, in fact, controls you, you can have some kind of power. *August 1993*

Iggy Pop was very much an influence in terms of the way he'd make up songs in performance. So ('Dirty Day') is really U2 in its most raw state. At the moment I'm toying with the idea of something that keeps flashing up in front of me when I hear the music, an image of a father giving surrealist advice to his son.

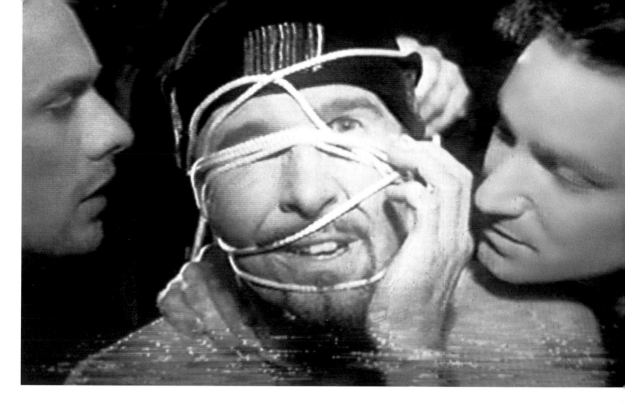

I also see Charles Bukowski in my head and the kind of advice he gives like, 'Always give a false name!' But whatever lyric I finally put to it, the music strikes me as very sad. What I'm saying there is 'Make it better, son.' The feeling I get is that the father has fucked off, or something like that. Then again it may end up being about Gorbachev! But what you're hearing there is the base of what will probably become a song, and the creative process is very much dictated by the atmosphere the band originally got while improvising. That's what'll dictate the kind of lyric the song finally has.
August 1993

**Now, even though ('Daddy's Gonna Pay For Your Crashed Car') has been heavily processed, the point is it was written through that process, rather than written as a blues then put through the technological mix. It was written back-to-front, as it were.
Yet to me it's definitely a blues song for the Nineties, as true to its roots as a song could be. *August 1993***

Edge has a list of things there, one following the other.
('Numb')'s kind of arcade music, but at base it's a dark energy we're tapping into, like a lot of stuff on 'Achtung Baby'. And, here, I use my Fat-Lady voice that I used on 'The Fly.' There's a big fat mamma in all of us! But you need that high wail against the bass voice because the song is about to overload, all those forces that come at you from different angles and you have no way to respond. It's us trying to get inside somebody's head. So what we're trying to do is recreate that feeling of sensory overload. *August 1993*

For us, it's a new way of working. We've been taking audio-visual loops and working with them. That drum loop ('In Cold Blood') comes from the scene where an 11 year old boy plays the drum at the 1936 Olympic Games. And we're going to be using that loop, in the actual stadium where that boy played, in Berlin. That's going to be a very eerie moment, because that boy could still be alive, I suppose... I will be standing in front of a 12 foot by 12 foot television image of the child playing the drum. *August 1993*

At the moment I don't know what it will look like in the end,
but we've worked with lots of video artists from the States and
Europe. Some of the stuff we do now is pertinent to what's
happening not just in Germany but all over Europe – I'm talking
about the new fascists. With 'Zooropa' we're trying to follow
the roots of the Berlin Dadaists and use humour to mock the devil,
as it were.

We're taking this machismo aspect of fascism and poking fun
at it. 'Cause we have it everywhere, even here in Ireland. We don't
know exactly what we have in mind. We're just experimenting.
There is not an exact philosophy of Zoo TV, it draws on whatever is
in the air at the time, whatever is being transmitted – that's what
ends up in the show.

Certainly at the moment I'm quite taken with a lot of the
Dadaists that came out of Germany in the 1930s, because there
are parallels between our time and that time. I'm also very
impressed by John Heartfield, who recently had an exhibition
in Dublin. But the Cabaret Voltaire people I really love. Because
the point is that the new fascists – rather like our own fascists,
the Provos – rely a lot on fear. And humour and laughter, to me,
is the proof of the presence of freedom.

The Dadaists, for example, were powerful in their time
because they had the ability to unzip the pants of the starched
trousers of these fascists and mock them. And they were outlawed
because of that. And I really feel there is a lot to be learned
from that. I've certainly learned a lot from that, philosophically
and in terms of expressing myself through our art. The potential for
subversion in humour is something new to U2. *August 1993*

**To be honest, I'm not completely sure what a lot of the
songs are about, they just... arrived. There's certainly an evil
feel to things like 'Daddy's Gonna Pay For Your Crashed Car'.
That song could be about dependency or something
more sinister. It's an electronic blues, my Robert Johnson
thing. Flogging the soul to Satan.** *September 1993*

('Lemon' looks at) the power of imagination, the mind taking
off in two different directions – in a Studio 54, Disco Duck setting.
The falsetto was completely natural. I've always felt there was a
fat woman trying to burst out of me. Don't know what Freud would
make of that! *September 1993*

**I'll tell you a funny thing, that song started out an Al Green
soul thing... that's so dark and deep that I don't think we want to
know what it's about.** *On 'The First Time', September 1993*

When we start records, Edge is a slow starter. He's not quick
to be enthused about a project. But at the end, when everybody
else is fading, he's the guy who's up all night for weeks. I mean, I'm
allergic to the studio after a few weeks. We wanted to acknowledge
the baby-sitting that Edge does. *On crediting the Edge as producer,
October 1993*

**One of the things that worked about this record is that
it was so quick. Edge is so good with the screwdriver, but we
didn't give him much time to use it – which was great.
He had more of an overall picture because he wasn't so taken
up with the details.** *October 1993*

Passengers: Original Soundtracks I

Brian Eno has been our producer for many years and it
was really nice to be in a band where he got to take the shit.
It's a very unusual record that we've just made with Brian.
He has an extraordinary musical imagination and we've learned
a lot from him over the years. Usually he takes the role as
irritant, he's somebody in the studio who stirs it up and has to
make it work. This time around he didn't have any other
responsibilities other than just being right on it, and we are
happy to be in his backing band. There is some interesting
material and it's a real trip of a record. It won't be for everybody
and this is not a rock record. It's a sort of late night on
a fast train.

It's about a beauty pageant. You know, the song's not saying
'Things are really bad in Sarajevo, please give us some money and
I'll take a cut.' *On 'Miss Sarajevo'*

Mother Records

John Lydon is very interested in traditional music.
I'm ringing him later on to talk about Dublin and being involved
in a record we want to make in Mother. Maybe produce it or
just be involved, because he would be the complete antithesis
of these traditional Irish musicians, and bringing the two of
them together with Mother acting as a middleman – it could
be incredible. I would like to see his ideas. *May 1981*

(Before Mother) there was nothing or nobody you could turn
to for advice. Obviously people like Bob Geldof and Phil Lynott,
God bless him, were there to help you out if they could, and
I remember Adam ringing Phil up one morning at about 8 o'clock
and asking him something about a recording contract! But that
was it! Hopefully now people don't feel that same lack of help
and that same pressure to leave the country before they're really
ready for it. *February 1986*

Mother actually had what you might call a false start
because we released the 'In Tua Nua' single about 18 months
ago and then did nothing else. But that's the way we want it.
It's not meant to be a record company or a label that brings out
stuff regularly and ties bands to contracts or anything like that.
It's just a bit of a leg-up in that really early period when most
bands here can't even get a single out. If a record company then
comes along after that and signs up the group, then fine.
February 1988

The Shows

In Concert

I'm like a clown, calling people to the stage... it's like
putting a magnet to iron filings, drawing them in. And once they
are in position, you can feed them, give them what you have.
We give and people look, and we give all... and that can affect
people's emotions; so we get a sensitive audience, people who are
aware. You see, I might be a hero on-stage, but off-stage I'm an
anti-hero. So you've got this hero image, which is rock'n'roll,
and the reality, where I meet the fans afterwards and I can't talk
'cause I get embarrassed. *November 1979*

**We felt sometimes when we were on-stage that we had a
spark because people were reacting, even when we knew only
four chords. We thought that even though we were technically
lacking, we had a spark. *June 1980***

You learn a lot about each other. Sometimes you're in a dressing
room before you're going on-stage and it's another city and another
town and maybe Larry turns around and says, 'Just another gig.'
And you pick him up by the scruff of the neck and knock him against
the wall and make him realise that this is what we are here for.
We are not here to give second best. And Larry himself will do it
to me as well. So we've learned to pull each other up when one
of us is getting lazy. And it's that struggle against that sickness or
that illness that actually makes this a very special gig. It's all in
your attitude. *May 1981*

**The concert in the RDS was the most successful concert of its
size I've ever been at in Dublin. There was such an atmosphere
of celebration, from the front rows to the back. That kind
of feeling between band and audience always leaves me
breathless. *January 1982***

Our belief in the people who come to see us is very strong.
That's what's important about our relationship with our audience.
February 1982

**Your knees go weak, your adrenalin starts to go crazy,
your bones just seem to rattle and blood shoots up your veins.
You think, 'Right, there is something about this band.'
*February 1982***

One thing I'm into is the type of people who are into us.
They're prepared to give, they're a reaction-orientated audience.
It's everything that we wanted when we were a garage band.
We wanted that total thing, people just up. *February 1982*

**I see working on the road like this a real learning
process. Every stage has a different sound and a different place.
Coming from a very small place like Ireland and going on out
into the world I feel privileged. And the only way to get things
across is to take it to these countries and give people a chance
to make up their own minds. *February 1982***

The only way our music and that of bands associated with us
is going to be heard, played on the radio out here, is by touring –

and it'll open the way for other bands. We go into stations and we shout our mouths off about bands that we think are good. *February 1982*

When people come through the doors at one of our gigs there's a tension there – then when we play there's a kind of unity takes over. People walk out drenched in sweat, excited, talking to each other. February 1982

I don't like music unless it has a healing effect. I don't like it when people leave concerts still feeling edgy. I want people to leave our concerts feeling positive, a little more free. Things might look very gloomy but there is always hope. *February 1983*

I was at this gig once in Ireland, and I was in the Gents trying to have a pee and there was this guy standing behind me staring and I just couldn't get it to happen. Anyway, I finally did, so just as I'm leaving he turns to me and says, 'Stage fright, eh Bono?' November 1984

I think people in the audience know more about the people in the band than everyone gives them credit for. People in the press sometimes want to capture a side of a personality and I think sometimes I'm portrayed in a very one-dimensional way but… I think the music is better than the musician and the audience is better than the journalist. I'm working on this thing that they know about these things, they know about music, as a mass, they know. *November 1984*

We all left school completely uneducated. Touring has been our way of learning. It upsets me when I see U2 portrayed in the press as touring, the pressure, the penance. I enjoy looking out of the coach window and seeing Denver Colorado or the run from Edinburgh to Glasgow. I mean, talk to Echo and The Bunnymen, to Simple Minds… these are the bands that are touring, we're not bored by it. This is not a penance. October 1984

We're still really travelling musicians, it's just that we have buses now, and computer mixing desks. *November 1984*

When security men start on the band then you start to wonder what you're doing on a stage. As it happens, I won't have them turning on the audience and that's what started the row. After bouncers attacked the band on-stage at Radio City Music Hall, December 1985

The 'War' thing, they were symbolic gestures, that's all. The white flag… I was sick of the green, white and orange, I was sick of the Union Jack and the Stars and Stripes. I wished that the colour could be drained from them and just leave the white flag. And I felt that a lot of people wanted that to be said – a lot of people who were in our audience. It was something very, very simple and the anger that came out at that time… anger is a very dangerous thing in the hands of a man like myself! It can come across that I'm angry with the audience, angry at them. It's always us with U2, I never write songs about 'you' or 'they.' It's 'us', it's 'we', it's 'I.' Always. It's a big difference. *November 1984*

I've never been to a U2 concert so I just can't think why anyone would want to come. But I'm very glad they go. May 1985

For me to sing on-stage, the only way I can do it is if I'm really committed to it and if I sense anything less than complete commitment from the others, then I get very antagonistic towards them and occasionally this has led to a bit of a fracas. Some people come to see U2 and expect to see me in saffron. *March 1987*

I always resented the stage, as something that would try and contain us and the music so I'd jump off it or climb the walls. But it ended up looking wrong, like I was coming down off the pedestal to the masses. *March 1987*

I've decided words speak louder than actions. I've got to put actions behind me. I always resented being on a stage, I always resented the barrier between me and the audience, and this led to that infamous gig in Los Angeles where I ended up falling off the balcony and a riot ensued and people could have got hurt. The band took me aside backstage and said, 'Look, you're the singer in a band, you've just got to get up there and sing. People in the audience understand the situation. You don't always have to remind them that U2 aren't stars to be worshipped – they already know that.' *March 1987*

We want our audience to think about their actions and where they are going, to realise the pressures that are on them, but at the same time not to give up. *1987*

When I started the year I had a chin I preferred, two shoulders that worked, a voice that could sing and most of my sanity. 1987 (has) been like going on Magic Mountain. You don't really want to do it, yet you still get on and it's completely dark inside. I've thought of a few chicken exits along the way this year. Particularly when I busted my shoulder. Dealing with 50-70,000 people is hard enough with two arms! In Boston I stopped the show and offered people their money back. I've felt like that a lot. There's been times when I've gone up to the promoter and said, 'Listen, this has all been a big mistake. Let's call the whole thing off.' *December 1987*

U2 attract an audience of all sorts. When we played in the United States, college professors came down to do a thesis on the Edge's guitar sound; we have people who like U2 'cos they think Larry Mullen Jnr looks like Jimmy Dean; we have people who like U2 'cos they think I'm John Paul II. We have everybody at U2 concerts. *1988*

You must not look down on someone just 'cos they are 14 years old. When I was that age I listened to the music of John Lennon and it changed my way of seeing things, so I'm just glad that 14 year olds are coming to see U2 rather than group X. *1988*

It can take a long time to re-adjust after a tour, you get what's known in nautical terms as 'the bends.' It's a sort of decompression that's necessary and it can fuck up a lot of people. I imagine that has happened to a lot of people who had success very quickly and find it very hard to ever come home, but, er I managed.

The stage is but a platform shoe after all – all it does is make us look bigger. I think dressing up as the devil was great and I enjoyed every minute of it. In fact I miss the old bird. It was an amazing thing actually, a woman called Eunice Schreiber who set up the

Special Olympics, she's one of the Kennedys and an Irish American, I suppose, she came to one of our shows, and she's 70 something or other.

She used to always come and see U2 shows, and she's very up on Irish politics, literature, in fact anything anywhere. She's a pretty sharp lady and she said to us after the show, 'You know, I used to go to the U2 shows and I just saw this band of angels and tonight I saw these devils as well as the angels on-stage. I think I liked it better. It's a fairer fight.'

We'll come back if we're still enjoying playing. It may sound selfish, but we play live a lot, and the world does seem to be getting bigger and you want to see new places. You want to go to South America, you want to go to Poland. *April 1992*

On-Stage Personalities

I can't quite remember whose idea it was. All I know is that Larry looked like some sort of porn star, Edge looked like his sister Jill, Adam hasn't taken the dress off and I looked like Barbara Bush. *On dressing in drag*

What we did with Zoo TV was, again, just a way of stopping me being placed as one person because you have to accept the bold type and the caricaturing that goes on when you become a big band and have fun with it and create these alter egos. I mean, we weren't parodying at all, you know, these were other sides of myself. The snake oil salesman, the Devil, The Fly, the Mirrorball Man, it was also a way of sending out decoys in a way, because, deep down, I'm still a really nice guy... Honest.

For me, MacPhisto is sort of sad, bad, not so funny but might be. It's like taking the rock jerk that The Fly is and – if you're going to play him – take him to his logical conclusion, which is when he's fat and playing Las Vegas. It's a book-end to the funny and fucked-up swagger of The Fly. *1993*

It's a language of scale, of surface – The Fly needs to feel mega to feel normal. One of the lines that didn't make it into the song 'The Fly' was that 'taste is the enemy of art.' There's a point where you find yourself tiptoeing as an artist, and then you know you're in the wrong place. It's like you have a rule book, but you don't remember where you got it. And along with that being true of the music, it can become true in a wider sense. I felt like I didn't recognise the person I was supposed to be, as far as what you saw in the media. There's some kind of rape that happens when you are in the spotlight, and you go along with it. *On his stage character The Fly, February 1993*

I always thought of The Fly as a meltdown kind of guy. I don't want to put too much emphasis on this character, but you gotta find new ways of saying the same things, you really do. I don't think it's a contradiction to find yourself on the beach at a nuclear power plant wearing those sunglasses. I think it is very surreal, and it was amusing to us even then. We were aware of how ridiculous it was. *February 1993*

I'd often found the sort of neon-light aspect of sex very funny, the leather and lace aspect. It wasn't a sexuality that I particularly related to, but it does seem a dominant sexuality. It's the one used to sell the products, and it's the one on

every corner, and so I got into it, and it's great! It's just
something I'm trying to understand, and I understand it a lot
better having dressed up as a con man for the past year.
On his stage character MacPhisto, February 1993

Live Aid

I remember being as high as a kite on what was going on...
It was as good backstage as it was front of stage. To have people
whose music you grew up on come up to you and offer their
support to what you were doing was amazing. *March 1987*

**For Bob Geldof, the sight of little bits of black plastic actually
saving lives was something of a shock. He had always thought
of pop music as something wonderful in itself, but nothing more
than that. But I wasn't quite as taken aback by the success of it
all. The Sixties music that inspired me was a part of a movement
that eventually helped to stop the Vietnam War and there is
no reason why contemporary music cannot have a similar
importance. *March 1987***

I remember getting carried away with myself on-stage. I forgot
it was a tight 15-minute thing on TV and I thought it was just U2
playing. As a result we didn't get to do 'Pride', and one song went
on for seven minutes because I saw someone getting squashed
down front and I was wanting to go down there. I wanted some
sort of gesture that included the crowd because they seemed as
important to me as the people behind the stage.
    The next few days were the blackest depression! I saw
the TV film back and I thought I'd made a big mistake, misjudged
the situation. I thought that's it, leave the group. This thing where
I was ending up in the audience had gone so wrong for me. I didn't
mean to do it at Live Aid. After that, I went out and drove for days.
I couldn't really speak to anyone. This whole thing of whether
I wanted to be in a band or not came back to me. At Live Aid the
whole question of Africa and the idea that millions were dying
of starvation brought back the stupidity of the world of rock'n'roll...
and when I got back I found people were saying the bit they
remembered was U2. *March 1987*

**I met a sculptor, a man in his fifties or sixties, and he was
working on a piece, a bronze, and he'd been watching his TV,
the Live Aid thing, and he described it all by saying that
there was a different kind of energy coming off the TV set.
The figure he was doing was of a man, a naked man, bent over,
and he called it The Leap. He said to me he was trying to
capture the spirit of the day, but the part of it he wanted was
our part, the U2 piece. I thought to myself, if a person who's so
removed from rock'n'roll can understand that, maybe it wasn't
such a big mistake. *March 1987***

I'd say Live Aid was the most extraordinary thing we've done.
I got a lot of shit from the band because I jumped off the stage and
instead of playing three tunes we only played two and I thought,
yeah, you're right. But I got carried away which I sort of see as my
job actually. But I can't walk out on a stage unless I believe it's
going to be the best of my whole life. It makes me physically ill to
walk out sometimes because I know it has to be the best. When
you're on tour for a long time it gets harder and harder to pull off.
So you have to believe that it has to be the next concert, otherwise
you just go home.

Zoo TV

**Zoo TV gets its energy from turning a stadium into a
living room with TVs with very personal songs on a huge PA.
Metal guitars, dance grooves, trash art, something for all the
family, something to annoy everyone. The more contradictions,
the better. It's like having one hand on the positive terminal,
the other on the negative... that's the energy of Zoo TV.**

I love this satellite thing. I love beaming across borders.
That's what U2 is about. And on the end of 1989 – literally,
on New Year's Eve, the turn of a decade, we put on a concert in
Dublin, our home town, in Ireland. And we – it was a radio concert
that went out all across the Soviet Union, and Eastern Europe.
And we printed, in Soviet magazines, the covers to the bootlegs they
were going to make from the concert. I think 500, or you know –
some ridiculous amount of people – 500 million people tuned in.
At that moment we got the idea for Zoo TV. *March 1992*

**We were all just a bit taken aback by the idea that you can
just transmit a concert on radio. And so Zoo TV is the visual
equivalent, you know. We can broadcast the show, all around
the world. We haven't done yet, and it's something we're
working up to. But it got us in – we got excited about doing
what we had done with radio – on television. *March 1992***

It is pretty dizzy. Just the kind of media overload we all experience and also the feeling that you can feel the ground beneath you giving way. There's a kind of confusion that is great for a rock'n'roll band to play with. We got very excited about working with all the stuff that was out there. I mean, a simple device like a telephone, that you would have on stage, is probably something that could not have occurred to Elvis, but you know, I just think that in the Nineties it's just amazing – you can just pick up a phone… you can ring the White House… or, you know, Allesandro Mussolini, the great dictator's grandchild who seems to be carrying on in the old boy's shoes and you can have 70,000 people singing 'I just called to say I love you' on the phone. Or play with televisions and beam in the advertisements, you know, whatever it is that day that happens to be going on.

Zoo TV just seemed like a way of being on tour for two years and not getting bored. At the same time as mocking, we are milking it, and enjoying it, kinda surfing on this media tidal wave of information. Some extraordinary stuff, like this Sarajevo broadcast which was hard to continue the show after, and some soap operas and ads. You know, and using the hard cut logic, that is everyday TV. Our everyday experience of watching Rwanda and what's going on there and then channel surfing in to EastEnders, and we do it, and that was the energy of Zoo TV.

This is technology we can abuse. Therefore we can make rock'n'roll into something new, instead of trying to pressure it, instead of trying to put a glass case around it. *December 1992*

I don't know what we're going to do in Europe yet. We're gonna re-work the show somehow. But we also want to put a record out soon, and there isn't time to do everything. I don't know what's gonna happen at the park. I'll be happy if… if our regular crowd that we played to on Tuesday night turns up, ha ha. We might even start a residency. *December 1992*

You've got to remember I was dressed as the devil, so The Satanic Verses just seemed right, I guess. It was more important than that. Salman Rushdie's position is more than just as a standard. The idea of freedom of speech, something we just accept as a given, isn't so in a lot of cultures. Particularly with rock'n'roll music and rap groups I think it's very important, that people have the right to be able to say whatever they want to say even if I don't like it. So Salman Rushdie's dilemma is closer to rock'n'roll than you might think. Plus I think he has behaved with enormous grace under pressure and with humour and wit and it must have scared the shit out of him to be on-stage at Wembley Stadium with the devil.
On bringing Salman Rushdie on-stage

People don't go away humming the video. We make the music more important by contrast to the barrage of images because after a while at Zoo TV you can't see anything.

Zoo TV is about contradictions. It's all about those instincts – we have all of them. *October 1993*

I've said it before, but there were reports of egomania, and I just decided to become everything they said I was. Might as well. The truth is you are many people at the same time, and you don't have to choose. It's like Edge describes me as 'a nice bunch of guys.' *February 1993*

We used to have a thing about our image: what image? We don't have an image. We're just playing with images, like the desert or whatever, and we dress in a way that's sympathetic to the music, but it's not an image. And finally, I just said, 'Fuck it, maybe it is. In fact, if it is, let's play with it, and let's distort it and manipulate it and lose ourselves in the process of it. But let's write about ourselves in the process of it, 'cos that's what's happening to everybody else on a smaller scale anyway. *February 1993*

We're right in the middle now, but the music… the music tells you what to do, and in the end that's what you gotta do. The music tells you what clothes to wear, it tells you what kind of stage you should be standing on, it tells you who should be photographing you, it tells you who should be your agent. You might see the glasses as a mask, but Oscar Wilde said something like, 'The mask tells you more about the man.' Something like that. But it's always the music that tells you what to do. And so if I want to take the glasses off, I just gotta change my tune. *February 1993*

We were travelling through Europe with this mad machine. We had been asked to play in Sarajevo, in a shelter, and we were trying to organise it. Then the people who invited us didn't want us to play because it was dangerous, not just for us, but for the people in the audience or in the queue outside. They thought it would become a turkey shoot. So the idea instead was to have unmediated talks with people… I think that's really interesting. It's one of the reasons why I thought it would be good to be here tonight… I'm sure that rock stars piss people off and now is the time, if you have a problem (audience laughter). We're here in Swansea and we – fight it out.

I danced every night under a mirror ball with a young lady from the Zoo TV crowd. Every night during 'Love Is Blindness'. They were amazing. I love it so much. Some nights I fell in love. I never really spoke to these people, but that's okay. *January 1995*

When we came off the Zoo TV tour we thought we could go into a decompression chamber and sort of come out the other end normal. We thought we could live a normal life and then go back on the road this summer. But it turns out that your whole way of thinking, your whole body has been geared towards the madness of Zoo TV. So our feet didn't touch the terra firma when we got back to Dublin. I met Edge and asked if he was feeling any better. He said he wasn't, so we decided to put the madness on a record. Everybody's head was spinning, so we thought: 'Why not keep that momentum going – instead of standing on dining tables at nine o'clock and throwing fruit around the restaurant?'
    Somebody said to me a while ago: how does your ego stand being in a band, how does it survive being a rock'n'roll star? And I thought that was one of the smartest things anyone had ever spotted about rock'n'roll. People think it's the opposite, that it pumps up your ego. I think it explodes your ego. It blows it out into fragments and that's why so many people who do what I do are so fucked up. So what U2 decided to do, with 'Achtung Baby' and the tour, is to explode our egos, publicly. Blow them up, in the billboard sense and in the sense of saying,

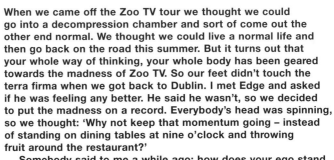

'Look, these are all the things we are.' So when I say that
rock'n'roll is ridiculous in the sense that people like U2 are paid
so much money to do all this, to play in a playpen, I mean it!
August 1993

How did I de-Zoo myself? I turned my television off. It was simple.
My white dot has receded out of view. There was nothing left.
The transmission had well and truly run its course. *February 1995*

Rock'n'Roll
(But I Don't Always Like It)

It's truly incredible. It's an incredible area to be getting involved in. Pop music... Phew! *March 1980*

The most powerful music is created naturally. It is not forced at all. It just comes out. *September 1980*

There's a lot of Johnny Rotten's bastard children running around the streets. They've been sold into bondage and it saddens me to see them because they've been sold the image of violence and now they've turned it into the reality of violence. *February 1981*

A band should have a personality of its own, and if a band's personality is dominated too much by one person, then it's bad for the band. On another level, a band like Spandau Ballet is totally direct and pointed. That's so boring because you see it all in one go – clothes, fashion, hair and that's it. There's nothing to discover, no mystique, no charm, no personality. *February 1981*

I'm not sure about Crass, but it's their supporters that worry me. With their Crass sew-on stickers. And their Crass logos on their leather jackets. I don't know, I don't like anything in uniforms. *May 1981*

That old cliché of rock'n'roll rebellion is a joke at this stage. It's so conservative you could actually write a rule book on how to behave as a rock'n'roll rebel. And I think rebellion starts with your own heart. I think going out and getting pissed and dyeing your hair red is not necessarily any indication of menace at all. *February 1982*

The Who Live At Leeds was a very important record in my life. *February 1982*

I don't think there's a lot of rock'n'roll about. I see rock'n'roll as an emotional, sweaty thing. *February 1982*

Punk was supposed to be a revolution, but it wasn't a real one. It was contrived in many ways, manipulated into a fashion thing. But we believed it. Punk rock fired us into trying to get music back to its roots. And I'd like to see a lot of the garage bands in America revolt. There has to be a garage band revolution. *June 1983*

You could say that The Sex Pistols were the ultimate designer rock'n'roll group. They were assembled with a view toward subversion. It wasn't like The Beatles, where John called round to Paul's house. It was more like Malcolm (McLaren, The Sex Pistol's manager) made phone calls. But at the same time they made a wonderful big, and nasty noise, and it woke me up. There was a cynicism and a manipulation involved in some of those punk groups, and we were blind to that. For us, it was true.

There's too many people hiding behind their haircuts. The cocktail mentality. The star trip is more in vogue now, with the kind of wallpaper bands, than it was with ELO and Zeppelin and all those. It seems the whole gloss thing is so strong now, and in '76 we maybe naively at 16 had the belief that music is more than that. We wanted a gut-level reaction, an aggression, a heartbeat. *June 1985*

Sado-masochism is not taboo in rock'n'roll but spirituality is. *1985*

I'm not anti-drink... all of us drink occasionally. But I don't think we're involved in what I call rock'n'roll masturbation, which is that you are in a band, you get wrecked with other bands, and it gets in the papers, and everybody laughs, ho, ho...!

If Jimi Hendrix walked into a modern A&R office I don't think he'd get the red carpet. He'd be shown the door. *March 1987*

I listened to the Stooges' Raw Power in the last few weeks. If you want to do heavy music, listen to that. Just these guys in a room. They were just what they sounded like. *March 1987*

It's not my place to comment on The Cult, but they've owned up to the point that Led Zeppelin I is an interesting record. It was almost unsaid that Led Zeppelin has made some music of merit. That's part of the claustrophobia. Let's forget forms. I just think rock'n'roll has to open itself up to the last 25 years. *March 1987*

Reading Robert Palmer's book on the blues, where he talks about bluesmen tying bits of metal onto their guitars to make them buzz, long before Jimi Hendrix – the noise and the buzz is all part of the sound you hear. When you go to a club you hear the sound mixing itself. The guitar and bass and drums all bleed into each other. The traditional way to make records is to separate those sounds into compartments and assemble them back. Along the way, they've lost a sense of soul and a spirit of performance. That was something that was very much on our mind. *March 1987*

An abuse of any tradition can be a bit wrong, writing weepy bedsit songs on a Spanish guitar – any amount of people will not get it right. But some will. I prefer people to try and fail, in a way, than to be constantly caught up in the Eighties and modern pop. I like to think to myself – what would Jerry Lee Lewis have done with a drum machine, if he'd been able to programme? It would have been amazing. Don't bow down in front of all the gadgets. *March 1987*

I think that over 25 years of rock'n'roll music it's redefined itself every few years. In the Seventies an understanding of high power was developed and absorbed, as folk music had been in the Sixties. The end of the Seventies brought an understanding of the spirit of rock'n'roll and the power of three chords, and then the Eighties has brought a fresh understanding of rhythm. To only listen to one era, to one period, is a big mistake. Surely, people should be buying Fifties records now. *March 1987*

You read about the excesses of the rock'n'roll stars of the Seventies – driving Rolls Royces into swimming pools. Well that's better than polishing them, which is the sort of yuppie pop ethic we've got in the Eighties. *November 1987*

What I find ridiculous about rock'n'roll in the Eighties is that it still thinks the Fifties rebel stance is relevant today. We all know that the spit-in-your-eye attitude is a marketing man's dream, so why do we bother? I've said this for years and I think people just thought the head had fallen off the shoulders, but I actually think U2 are radical. That's the word for what U2 are doing because it's different from the norm. *December 1987*

Have you heard Million Dollar Quartet, the bootleg that everyone's heard of, but no one has actually heard? I've got a copy. It's where all of them are standing around this piano, singing gospel songs. It's just unbelievable. Real rock'n'roll. There's this idea that U2 are nothing to do with rock'n'roll, but we're much closer to the confusion at the heart of it. December 1987

I don't think that in the Eighties we were a rock'n'roll band; I think we were the loudest folk band on earth, but that now we're a rock'n'roll band.

I think rock'n'roll re-invents itself every few years and in the Seventies, I suppose power was the dominant force: the distorted guitar, amplifier, feedback, The Who and so on. Then there was The Sex Pistols and punk, and later funk, with people rediscovering the rhythm of rock'n'roll. And in the Eighties we're back to songwriting and the power of words. *1988*

U2 had become a bit like tunnel vision, and I think we had to take our blinkers off and take a look around us. If you see a film like Paris, Texas and hear the music of Ry Cooder, then pick up his records; then you get into the Delta and into the blues and then you discover the work of John Lee Hooker.

From there I got into Willie Dixon, and people like that. Actually, I met Willie Dixon's son in Chicago, in a blues club, and went up on-stage with him. I'm only just discovering and I find that whole gospel/blues confusion really interesting. I don't want to be overpowered by these influences, but there's a whole world out there and I'm just beginning to see what's going on. 1988

I have a great curiosity. That explains everything, probably. I'm curious about a musical past that we don't have. I want to see things for myself. I want to experience it first hand. I'm attracted to the sort of people you ought not to hang about with. But I need to be with them, not to lose sight. There are two ways of doing this. Either through your own eyes or through those of artists who have walked that way. *1988*

Press conferences are a bit like an obstacle course. You're not going to start talking about meanings or messages 'cos it makes you sound a right prat, so you just have to be a bit glib and try and dodge your way through. 1988

Rock'n'roll has always been full of shit. The whole idea of sex, drugs and rock'n'roll is a cliché. Someone has to put a bullet into its head. *September 1988*

Rock'n'roll has always had a little bit of irreverence. At the same time, I'm more reverent about music, about the spirit of it, about what's at the heart of rock'n'roll. December 1988

I'm not stupid. I'm aware of the futility of rock'n'roll music, but I'm also aware of its power.

As a musician you have to be prepared to take your clothes off.

Why is it all so cut up and compartmentalised? Why can't
we have it all! Why can't rock'n'roll dance like Elvis Presley, sing
like Van Morrison, walk like The Supremes, talk like John Lennon,
roar like The Clash, drum like Keith Moon and play guitar like
Jimi Hendrix? Why?

**The world of rock'n'roll is as black as a mine but you
could find a jewel down there to make it all worthwhile.**

If you gave a pop star a shit pile of dough, and he refuses
to self-destruct, I think it's a bit wet. I think it's part of a deal,
if they don't die on a cross before 33 I'd ask for my money back.

**All art is contrived, musicians have always been shamen
I guess, or magicians. It looked like it wasn't that way, you didn't
see the hands move, but now showing how the trick is done is
the act.**

Stadium rock is a term that was developed to describe the
guitar bands of the mid-Seventies – bands who in terms of style,
content, and sound have much more in common with what's known
as grunge than with the Seventies rehash thing has nothing to do
with us, and I personally have had it up to here with all that
GGGRRRRRRRRRR stuff. It's so white, so male, so hormonal.

**I mean, rock'n'roll is ridiculous. You have to see that.
You have to know that. Rock'n'roll is, you know, ludicrous at
times. It's funny. I mean, four jerks in a police escort.
I mean – that's funny. *March 1992***

I think it's part of the job to provide some sort of jeopardy.
To be at least unreliable and at best, you know, human sacrifice and
self mutilation. It's cool to be concerned with the environment,
it's cool to have political attitude but only if it brings you close to
your real job as a firework. And the business of getting up on
the cross, I guess.

**I'm not sure that any artist/rock'n'roll band should be taken
too seriously. Time will tell if you are more than your moment,
but in our moment we are definitely the most interesting
rock'n'roll band on the planet.**

It's like a footballer's income. The money you get is unbelievable,
really, it's such a lie that rock'n'rollers live. I just think there must
be very few people in the music business, in terms of artists,
with money in the bank. Because they have it for a few years and
it's gone and they have to live for the rest of their lives kind of thing.

**I think it would be rude and ignorant to say money isn't
important to me because money is so important to a lot of
people because they don't have it and I know I have it and
I'm lucky and I thank God that I have money.**

Mystery and mischief are the essence of rock'n'roll.

**We used to broadcast what we believed in, now we
broadcast what we don't believe in. They're two sides of
the same coin, but one's a lot easier than the other.**

I don't look up to literature or down from it, I think it's part
of the spectrum, as is music, and they're mixed up in some
indefinable way.

**People see a suite in the top of a hotel in Chicago and think it
must be the most incredible place to be. But the more plush the
surroundings, the poorer you feel in spirit sometimes.**

I think it's fair to say you become attracted to the very
things you are afraid of. Our reaction to the media is more of a
Judo mentality, I mean you use the energy of what's coming
at you to defend yourself.

**Anton Corbijn's photographs are very powerful. They are
as much photographs of the music as they are of the musicians,
and that's why we like them.**

The difference between pop and rock'n'roll is that the pop star
gets the nose job.

**Often rock'n'roll music is a very narrow emotional band width.
It's simply, 'I want to shag you', and that's very high on my list of
agendas, but how I want to and why, and 'oh gosh, I'm married.'
You know, all those things that make it more interesting.**

Britain hasn't put out many great rock bands like The Kinks,
the Stones, The Beatles… because it had the potential, there have
been some great bands coming through, but they've been broken
up by, I suppose, a kind of small-mindedness that seems pervasive
to what's going on here. The Smiths, The Clash: great rock'n'roll
bands. They're not around. The whole idea that big is bad is really
dangerous. *April 1992*

**In America people said having Public Enemy on the bill
would affect ticket sales or there'd be riots. That hasn't been
the case. You don't have to agree with everything they have
to say but you've got to listen. *December 1992***

Friends, Rivals, Relations...

On Roy Orbison
I found him to be a very wise man; he had a lot to say.
He seemed to be a man who was incredibly surprised by his own talent – I mean, he had the voice of an angel – and well, now he is one. Roy was the finest white pop singer on the planet.
December 1988

On Gavin Friday
'Shag Tobacco' is a song by a guy called Gavin Friday and he's got an album out called Shag Tobacco. He's a kind of cabaret singer from the future, he's an extraordinary man and is one of my best mates and one of my biggest influences. I don't know if I could sing a song like that because it comes out of his experience and he brings it alive because of that. If I was to sing one of his songs I'd probably choose 'He Got What He Wanted But Lost What He Had'.

On Pete Wylie
Pete Wylie is the only person I know who can out-talk me.
He fills in the gaps where I have to take breaths. *February 1982*

On Madonna
I'm interested in anything she does. The music is a little off-the-shelf for me, but it's almost like the lack of personality in her music heightens the personality in her voice. *February 1993*

On R.E.M.
Sometimes I'd love to be in R.E.M. and talk about Athens or – who else would I like to be – I'd like to be somebody who talks about the Velvet Underground and their influence on us... there are all these things I want to talk about. *1989*

Michael Stipe's a great singer. He's kind of like a Bing Crosby of the Nineties, though, isn't he? He's a crooner. *February 1993*

On Bill Clinton
We were on tour and we got into the Ritz-Carlton in Chicago... He came round to my room next morning: we were all looking fairly rock'n'roll after the night before, but he just laughed out loud. He was very relaxed with it... We told him we weren't going to endorse him, that wasn't what we did, and if he got in what we'd be on his back for the next four years because there is an uneasy relationship between us and politicians. But he knew that. He got that. That's when I realised he's pretty cool. *February 1993*

On Donal Lunny/Common Ground
The Seventies threw up hard rock, punk rock and disco but none of them could budge The Bothy Band. Donal Lunny had his toes, never his head, in the sand and in the Eighties and Nineties kept Irish music from being traditional. *April 1996*

On Ian McCulloch

Ian McCulloch – I think I surprised him. I told him the truth about how I felt about him. That he was a good performer in a great band and that he deserves to be a pop star. I don't think he quite expected that. *May 1981*

On Clannad

I'll tell you why Clannad is so special. When they were only around 10 years old they went for miles knocking on people's doors, ancient isolated cottages far from anywhere, and they asked these people to sing them the traditional Irish airs. Some of these songs are hundreds, thousands of years old. They're part of the very fabric of Irish history. To me, at that age, wanting to keep tradition alive is something very special. *After recording a duet, 'In A Lifetime' with Irish folk group Clannad, 1988*

On The Pogues

I think the most radical thing about The Pogues is that you'll find a 60-year-old man in a pub singing one of their songs and fully understanding what it is all about, maybe more than his son does. The generation gap doesn't exist anymore. I know old men who are more interesting than their children or their children's children and I know people of 25 who are dead and they're just postponing their funeral till they're 70 or whatever. *1989*

On Keith Richards

It's interesting that when Keith Richards straps on a guitar, all the lines disappear from his face. But it's the lines that interest me more. I'm interested in people who have come out of something more than the pre-pubescent rock'n'rollers I was a part of. That was punk, that was spit-in-your-eye, that was, 'I don't know what the hell I'm talking about but I'm going to talk about it anyway.' That used to be the attitude I was interested in. Now I find these people far more interesting. *December 1987*

If Keith was 20 years old in the Eighties I don't think he would have got into junk, he wouldn't have been into heroin as rebellion. The Sixties were a different time and in terms of rock'n'roll it was the first time. People were dizzy with it and maybe it seemed the right thing to do at the time or whatever. It is quite obvious it was the wrong thing to do because a lot of people died. Now we know that, but then they didn't. That was the generation that thought it could live forever; they thought they had immortal number plates on their car. *1989*

Keith Richards is the kind of person that sometimes gives the impression that he's in a world of his own over at the other side of the room, but he's actually very wide awake. He's a man with all the infamy and fortune anyone could want and it all means very little to him. The music is the all-important thing to him. Whether you like or dislike him isn't really the point. The important thing is that he hasn't taken the bait and been middle-classed out like so many others. *January 1986*

On Nirvana

I think it's good that Nirvana are on Geffen Records. I don't think they should be embarrassed by it. I think Kurt Cobain is a fine singer. I know the 'R.E.M. with a fuzzbox' argument, but I actually think they are an important group and they've got vitality and they should just do anything they want to do. The fact that they sell as many records as Madonna is great. You see, we've been there. There is a kind of Catholic guilt that can go with success, but I just hope some of these groups don't start tiptoeing.

I always felt it was our responsibility to abuse our position.
That was one of the ways we went into the sessions for 'Achtung
Baby'. Because we had been spoiled by success financially,
we had what Groucho Marx called 'fuck off money'. If you waste
that, you're a wanker, you don't deserve anything. At this point in
U2, we've made more money outside U2 than we ever did inside U2,
so there's only one reason for walking into a recording studio,
and there's only one reason for going out on tour, and that is to do
exactly what we want to do. *February 1993*

On BB King

You learn a lot watching somebody like BB King and going
back to those early R&B records. That was the thing we needed,
I think. That's what was missing in the puzzle for U2. It's a different
place that was necessary for us to go in the light of the new
subject matter. You can't write songs about sex if you don't have
it in the music. *February 1993*

On Frank Sinatra

I don't know what I can do with that. I'm not going to croon
it next to him. I might talk. I want to spook it up, because those
Cole Porter songs are spooky. I don't know if you heard that
'Night And Day' thing we did (on Red Hot & Blue) – that's where
we connect with Cole Porter. They're spooky, fucked-up songs
of obsession. Some people perform them so fruity it's like whoa!
These are really dark pieces of work.

Miles Davis was a great appreciator of Sinatra's phrasing.
That turned me on to him, listening to him in a different way.
I've seen him about five times. We met him in Vegas – we went
backstage, and we were hanging out with him. It was like Rent-A-
Celebrity, and we were like gyppos, just knackers. Larry was talking
to him about Buddy Rich, who'd just died, and he didn't want
to talk about anything else. He came alive. You got the feeling that
maybe not a lot of people talk to him about music, and maybe
that's what he's more interested in.
*On recording 'I've Got You Under My Skin' for Frank Sinatra's
Duets album, October 1993*

Oasis v Blur

I love it all, they are both good writers and great songwriters…
(and) the girlfriend of the guy in Blur, she's got a great band, Elastica.
But I do think that when that guy Liam sings there is some sort of
ache, as well as the anger, and it's the ache that separates certain
music from others. 'Clever' has never been high on my list of
priorities for music. You have to be moved. It has to be magical,
it has to have that something else and in that sense he is a shaman
and his band are great.

On Britpop

There are some very interesting things happening over here
at the moment. All of these bands really want to go all the way;
unlike a lot of bands of the past, they want to be big like the Stones
and The Beatles and I think that's great because in the Eighties you
were hanged for such ambitions. The indie thing really knee-capped
rock'n'roll and nobody could own up to their ambitions.

When I joined the band, I wanted to be in the Stones or
Beatles or Who or Kinks. So what I really hope is that some great
bands come out of this and go all the way and enjoy the
momentum of that, because momentum is the real creative player
when you're in a band. The attitude of 'no, we only play clubs'
then 'OK, we'll play the theatres but we'll never play the arenas',
on to 'well, we'll play the arenas but we'll never play stadiums';

it just went on and it's happening in America now. It's the same
old crap and I just think, well, if you are a shy introverted person
you become a potter or something, you don't join a fucking
rock'n'roll band.

There were some really fine bands who seemed to shrivel
up and die because they were so religiously hip. I just hope that
Blur and Oasis really take on the world and win – fuck up the
mainstream, why don't *you?*

On Pavarotti
When we arrived at the airport he was waiting to pick us up
with five white limousines, five Mercs. The window came down and
the big man was sitting at the wheel and he asked us into his car
and drove us 15 miles to his house. The gates opened and we went
up this long drive and he parked the car... at the table! (Laughter)
He opened the door and said, 'pasta!' That's what did it for me!
On 'Passengers: Original Soundtracks I'

The Fame Game

What's it like to be a rock star? There must be people better
qualified to answer that. I think I'm a kind of part-time rock star.
We're probably the worst rock'n'roll stars ever, we've got all
the wrong equipment... these arms are stuck on the wrong way.
June 1985

I get people throwing too much responsibility on me.
People literally arriving to die on my front lawn. People coming
from all over the world to pinch a pair of y-fronts off my line.
July 1987

It gets boring to say that U2 are great. In Ireland, they've had
this for years. And then of course there's a lot more things going
for Dublin, and for Ireland, than U2. So when they have U2 rammed
down their throats, I don't blame them throwing it up now and then.
I also think it is a very healthy thing to be cynical about rock'n'roll
groups. I think it's particularly good to be cynical about the sort
of groups that aspire to the sort of things that U2 do. Because we
saw in the Seventies how rock'n'rollers got incredibly fat on their
acclaim, so I actually think it's a good thing. I do understand it,
although I obviously would prefer praise. *October 1988*

We couldn't care less about the success of our records at
this point. We've had one LP that sold so many records that we
don't have to worry about things like that again. We didn't
even worry in the first place, I must say. But we certainly don't
worry now. We're just after music. October 1988

Tour madness? Oh... it's like cabin fever... when you're on
tour for long periods of time. Listen, I've got the greatest job in
the world, and I'm totally overpaid for it, but that said, there are
times when no matter how beautiful your hotel room is, it doesn't
matter what hotel it is, at times you start to feel like a prisoner.
Sometimes it just brings the worst out of you. But after you come
back to your hotel room, it's a very lonely place. Even if your
mates are just down the hall from you, sometimes it's just a very
lonely place... that's what tour madness is. *October 1988*

We have two ways of dealing with our wealth.
We have what U2 does as a group – decisions that are made
collectively about income – and we have our own personal
responsibilities. Both we keep secret, and while that doesn't
absolve us from all the guilt of having a lot of money in a society
that doesn't have much, at least it makes us feel we're doing
something worthwhile with that money. There are still
contradictions to be tackled – but if I choose what I'm going
to tackle in a day, I mustn't put it before being in a band making
music. You know it's almost harder to give away money than
earn it because of the responsibilities involved.
**   From all the flak we get in this level from the middle class,**
we still have a huge working class audience. I would get more
flak in a pub in Foxrock than I would in the Ballymun House.
There, I think people feel 'well, it's his business.' And they know

we pay taxes and they know we make a lot of money for the country anyway. I mean, I don't mind paying taxes though I try to pay as little as I can, obviously – I prefer to equally distribute my wealth.
I think I've said before that I always felt rich.
When we were growing up in the Lypton Village gang, some of us had money, some of us didn't. I didn't notice. I was being supported by my mates, by Ali, by everything. But I'm not stupid. I know how to make money, and probably have some sense in that area, but I'm not interested in it for its own sake and never have been. You know, my old man laughs at me – he finds it hysterically funny 'cos I was never interested in money. He thinks this is evidence of God's sense of humour because I'm not that way. I'm probably greedy in other ways – possessive about people, maybe. *1989*

Most people out there have to bend over for a buck just to pay the rent or whatever, so it's horrible to see rock'n'roll stars doing it because they've got a shitload of dough anyway.
It's just embarrassing to see someone wrap their arms around a Coke can and kiss it for money when they don't need the money. It's not a big deal... I mean people that provide your gear, your strings on your guitar, that's always happened. So, we don't want to get too sanctimonious about it. But it's just where you draw the line. Also, for young bands, I can't blame them, if they want to appear as a sponsored act and they have no money... *April 1992*

We're in a really great position in a way because we can get away with things that bands not at our level can't get away with. It might be something like just releasing 'The Fly' and actually making American radio stations play it because it's the new U2 single. I mean sometimes small things like that can actually make a difference and it's good fun just challenging the accepted way of doing things.
Whatever it takes to get that bastard to number one.
And that's what it's about, it's abusing your position, that's what it is. No, (having it on release for just three weeks) wasn't our idea, it was the record company's idea – and it was a really good idea. I don't know, I just think that is a cool thing to get away... and that's our job, to abuse our position to get stuff on the radio that wouldn't normally get on the radio.
We've had some help and we're very pleased with it.
And it is cool that you're playing it and all the people are playing our records. We don't expect to get played at 7.30am, and the fact that we are I think is good – not only for U2, which it's very good for, but for the BBC because they don't look as asleep as they might do. *April 1992*

We don't have to (use any songs on commercials), I mean that's it... you don't have to do it. I always thought that was the deal, you know, there is some kind of deal between you and your audience, I mean they gave you the dough and say don't worry about where you're going on holidays and where you're going to live and all the rest, just give us the good music and don't do anything stupid. *April 1992*

The whole idea of dangerous is still rooted in the Sixties. What was dangerous back then is not at all dangerous now. The whole thing, this self-destruct thing, the whole sex and drugs and rock'n'roll, that's playing into the hands of the corporations. They just call it built-in obsolescence, you know, burn out some rock'n'roll star, find another one. That's all bullshit.

**Rebellion is a much more sophisticated thing now.
To be subversive is not to smash up your hotel room – your
record company will be very happy about that. You know if I
wanted to piss in a BBC cup here that might be very good
for record sales but it is not dangerous or rebellious. I actually
cannot believe that people still fall for the old shite. It's too easy.
I can't believe that people are still plugged into that idea of
rebellion. The things of the spirit are what is really rebellious...
that's what actually put people's noses out of joint right now
and not sex. Sex... corporations are built on that, it sells Pepsis,
sells Coca Colas, sells everything. We're shocked so easily,
it's sad.** *April 1992*

Anyone who needs 50,000 people a night to tell them they're OK
has to have a bit missing. And I do mean that in terms of your sense
of self, not necessarily in terms of sanity. And I don't think you start
out that way but, as with Elvis, it's a place you can get to easily.
August 1993

Into The Arms
Of America

Growing up in Ireland I was aware of America as a super-real
place. It was as though it didn't really exist. It might only exist on the
television and when I turned off the television America would just
disappear. When I got to America I found it was just as super-real as
it was on TV. I remember that TV was true to life. *1988*

In America we are a number one project for Warners.
They are bringing a huge machine into operation for us.
That can be a very ugly and frightening thing if you are not in
control of it. Because it can just spit you out. It can build you.
Or it can smash you down. We've actually retained control by
having the right people work for us. *May 1981*

A network is building up. In every state, English music papers
get through. College radio covers groups like U2, Scritti Politti,
Teardrop Explodes. Because radio is going to go out of fashion if it
doesn't wake up. I spoke to a radio programmer who said people
like Loverboy this year 'cos they sounded like Foreigner last year.
These are conservative times we're going through and nobody likes
'new'. It isn't a good word. *February 1982*

We love being here as far as playing is concerned.
The audience reaction is instinctive. There isn't much reading on
music. The only way people hear about things is by the radio,
which is very localised. You could be huge in Boston and people
won't have heard of you in Texas. *February 1982*

The Irish built America. *November 1984*

America is a very powerful place. You fight with it, you wrestle
with America. I always say there are two Americas, there's
one that's spelt Amerika and that's 48 channels, that's Ronald
Reagan, that's pistols and the Ku Klux Klan. But I'm interested
in America, which is open space, which is a new found land,
the cities and the people in the cities who come to see us play
and who I feel are extraordinarily open to our music and have
not got preconceived notions about the group and are not
as inhibited sometimes as audiences in other parts of the world.
November 1984

I had to stop our last show in New York because I was in the
middle of 'Sunday Bloody Sunday' and there was a party of people
giving it the 'Eff the British' line. So I stopped the show and said,
'Okay, it's all over, you're completely misreading this band.'
There's times in the show that I have to say that. At the time it
might not sink in, but afterwards as they take the train home,
as they walk through the streets and they're talking about it...
You know my feeling on this, I believe that in the mass there is a
collective understanding of what we're doing. But there are
exceptions to that. *January 1985*

**I remember our first gig in America, at the Mud Club in
New York, and these people from Premier Talent coming up
to us and saying, 'It's going to be interesting when you play
Madison Square Garden.' I mean, that was everything we were
against, and we were against playing these aircraft hangars
right up to the time I went to see Bruce Springsteen at Wembley
Arena. Now I enjoy these places – instead of a backdrop
of stained glass windows we've got people – that's it, people!
And we are making big music. When we start 'Pride', that floats
over the audience, and to confine it is living in a lie.**
June 1985

In America, you get all the mission from God people, the type
of ones that hear voices telling them to contact U2... Madness.
June 1987

**I sorta OD-ed on America. It's like, y'know, the guy in
Clockwork Orange, they pin his eyes back and on a huge screen
overdose him with ultra violet images... Hah! It still fascinates
me, the good and the bad, the cultural schizophrenia towards
America is a particularly Irish thing, y'know cos of our
relationship to it over the years. Plus as a writer you are filled
with these fleeting impressions, the madness of America
seeps through...** *June 1987*

There was a night in LA in the early part of the tour when we
had a death threat that the police were taking very seriously indeed.
Someone had sent the gun licence into the U2 offices and they
thought he had gotten into the venue. All of a sudden there were
all these cops on the stage which I really objected to. I never
thought that sort of thing would bother me and, when I went out,
it didn't. I just laughed it off, like The Blues Brothers – 'We're on a
mission from God and we ain't finished yet.' The second night came
up and the cops came up to us just before we were about to
go on and said they'd made a mistake. He was coming tonight!
Second time round I stopped laughing.
    Now, we get all kinds of racist jibes because we wrote a song
for Martin Luther King, or pinko jibes because we did the Amnesty
International Tour. Wherever you look we're a target for the loony
fringe. So the second night, we're on-stage and I'm singing 'Pride'
thinking, 'If someone is going to do it it will be during this number.
So I crouched down on the stage, shut my eyes and for a moment
the thought of this death threat crossed my mind. When I looked
up I just saw Adam standing over me, between me and the crowd.
It was a good, good moment... I never liked the bastard.
December 1987

**When I was on the West Coast I was almost allergic
to people for a while. Every time the phone rang I'd panic.
I just stayed in my room for days because I felt I was completely
used up. I was a commodity bought, sold and soon to be
redundant. I got over it soon enough, though. A few drinks and
a hamburger and I'm back with the human race again. It would
be really boring for me to moan about what should have been
the best year of my life.** *December 1987*

I think the only reason we get away with criticism of America is
that we love America. *December 1987*

**How on earth can I get America out of my system?
I can't get it out of my television!**

Elvis changed everything: the America I know was born in
1956 when Elvis appeared on the Merv Griffin Show – because
black'n'white music collided in this guy's spastic dance. He had
white skin and a black heart. What I love about America is the
fact that it's a melting pot of European and African culture
keeps it from going straight. I think what's really significant about
Elvis Presley and rock'n'roll culture is everything changed in America
after that – racism was broken down as significantly as it was
through the peace movement and MLK – not institutional racism,
but common racism. It was an extraordinary event: an explosion
took place.

Elvis ate America before America ate him.

We all live in America in the sense that you turn on the
television and it's America, as is a lot of the music we listen to...
America's bigger than just 700 million people over there.
As Wim Wenders said, 'America's colonised our unconscious' –
it's everywhere, so how can I get it out of my system?
November 1991

**The English preoccupation with 'big' is more to do with empire,
or the loss of it, than it has to do with music. They used to
have a big navy, big football teams, build big bridges with big
brains and did some wonderfully big things; certainly some
of the biggest rock'n'roll bands were British. But now it's all
'we're not big because we don't want to be'... I mean, cut the
crap and show us your willy, let's leave the small is beautiful
thing to the Japanese... who are much better at it. Rock'n'roll is
about being big. You know, momentum is one of the players
and if you want cottage industry – take up knitting. I just think
it's penis envy. Great Britain used to be America, and then it was
fine to be big, but now the small is beautiful thing is more
related to, I think, a fear of being American than anything else.**

I can't understand how a culture (British) that's thrown up some
of the greatest pop artists of the second half of the 20th century still
does refer to it sneeringly as 'pop music', and it's kind of held at
arms length, 'over there'. I think that so many of these people have
set fire to our imagination, to my imagination and turned me on
to thinking in ways that I couldn't explain in an hour. I don't think
that they have the same problem in the US and certainly not in
Ireland. It's either great or it's not great. Just because it's written in
a book doesn't mean it's higher or lower and I think you might suffer
a little bit from that in England. I think that's a great shame because
there are great writers but there are also great bands and great
music. In fact I just saw in the Sunday Times survey that people put
music at the top of the list of things that had the most impact on
their lives.

Ted Turner (CNN) is the new king of America.

U2 Can Save the World

Men of Peace

Martin Luther King wasn't a passive pacifist, he was a militant pacifist. People out there, if you can articulate something for a mass of people as you're singing, it might just be something like 'No more, no war.' Everyone feels like that. They don't go through every day thinking about it, but yet it's in there. Everybody's aware right now of the fact that there's an alliance between Ronald Reagan and Mrs. Thatcher, that there are missiles moving into Germany, but you're not aware of it on a conscious level are you? You don't wake up and think, 'Oh, another day that might be our last.' You don't think like that. *November 1984*

People think the reasons I'm attracted to Martin Luther King or Ghandi or Jesus Christ is that, in some way, I am a real man of God myself. In truth, the real reason that I'm attracted to these peaceful men is that I'm the guy with the broken bottle. I grew up that way and I despise violence, I despise the violence that's in me and that's why I'm attracted to men who have turned their back on it. *March 1987*

A real hero is John Hume, he is the man in there. He has been working the same groove for 20 years. He's the Martin Luther King of this moment, and I am sort of Old Testament and Californian enough to believe in atonement and karma, but I do think it is also very important for Britain because Britain has a lot to answer for in this regard. I think people want to throw off that baggage and I think it's really important to start again and start afresh. I think it would be great for Prince Charles to come to Ireland and actually say there has been a terrible tragedy here and we are part of it and let's try to work our way out of it. Something like that would do, I mean, what else are Royalty good for?

On Central America

In Nicaragua it's... well, it's the sexiest revolution I ever saw. Women in khaki uniforms standing on corners and... well, I don't like anyone with an Armalite rifle, but there they were standing there smoking cigarettes and looking like Miss World. *March 1987*

You can fall asleep in the comfort of your freedom. We can't right all the wrongs, but we can find people who can help to do it. If Amnesty are doing it, why not lend support to them? *March 1987*

I was drawn towards Central America through meeting René Castro (a Chilean artist). At first he didn't pay me much attention until he discovered the Amnesty connection. Amnesty saved his life. He'd been captured when Allende was killed and they had the military revolution. He was tortured.

He had a hole in his chest. They bored a hole in his chest.
He was in the stadium with Victor Jara when he had his fingers
cut off and then, eventually, was brutally murdered. Amnesty
International got him out and people from the Latin American
community came to our gigs and René Castro sent me some
of his paintings. And eventually I was asked to go to El Salvador
and Nicaragua. *March 1987*

I was asked to go there (Central America) and this whole world
opened up. I sat with the mothers of the dispossessed and they
showed me black and white photographs of how their children had
been sent home, dismembered. It was like a never-ending nightmare.
I saw bodies dumped out of the back of a van as I was going down
a motorway. A man who'd brought me round, being followed by
death squads. I saw villages being terrorised and bombed by fighter
planes while I was on the way to visit them. It seemed like years,
the weeks I spent there. It just makes Amnesty International seem
like a very good idea. *March 1987*

Going to Salvador... you could feel the malevolence from
the troops. It was awful. I was outside on my way to a village
and the village was bombed and it scared the shit out of me.
I didn't know which way to run. They were mortaring this village
and there were fighters overhead and this farmer says to me,
'No worry, ees over there.' He was going through it every day of
his life and he'd learned to live with it, whereas I was there
for just a few weeks and I was really concerned about number
one at that point. Troops opened fire over our heads while
we were there, just flexing their muscles, and I literally felt sick.
March 1987

On War

When I think of Vietnam, I think of two things; Hendrix playing
'Star Spangled Banner', and the photo of that child running after
a napalm strike. The things that affect me most about Vietnam
both happen to be conveyed through a creative medium, I think the
creative media, including rock'n'roll can make real the situation a
country finds itself in. *December 1987*

Information and communication, these are the currencies
of right now, money doesn't actually exist anymore, does it?
It exists as a concept, it exists on binary codes on microchips.
Modern wars are fought over ratings, it's not enough to win a
war, you have to look good winning it. It's the images that come
out of the war that count. This is where the US got it wrong
with Vietnam, and got it right with Baghdad. It was orchestrated
very well, it looked good that war, you didn't hear the bad stuff
until much later.
     The images we have of Vietnam are of that burning child.
Well there's a burning child right now just 200 miles from here,
in all likelihood, in Sarajevo. There is a massacre happening
as we speak. It's not in the paper, or on the media, and unless
we see those images, we won't react. I don't think it's a
coincidence that in the war in Bosnia there have been more
journalists killed than in the history of human conflict. There's a
price on the heads of journalists because those warlords know
that it's images that count. Words no longer communicate.

You know, all the prisoners aren't out and all the people who are starving aren't fed... so it goes on.

I know that these days to make the same point you have to be a little smarter and that's why we're going back to Sarajevo, for a moment – there was a real clue there. I was blown out by these Dadaists. The Dadaists, originally from Switzerland, grew up in response to National Socialism and the Nazis and they used humour. Humour is the best weapon and I think that, for instance, comedians are the real rebels in a sort of prophetic sense. They get away with shit that rock bands would be locked away for. I just think you've got to be smart about the way you go about making any points.

I can really understand the overwhelming majority deciding to take up arms against the system of Apartheid (in South Africa). I could really understand and relate to it – but I hope they don't have to do that. It would be better if it didn't have to happen that way. But I mean, there's another contradiction, another ugly contradiction of Ronald Reagan's America – that they would support the Contras to undermine a state like Nicaragua, which they see as illegal, and yet they make no effort to undermine the Apartheid system which they also say is illegal. *1989*

On Nuclear Power Plant in Sellafield

We live 130 miles from Sellafield in Dublin – it's a lot further to Downing Street as you might have noticed. It doesn't smell right here. It's pretty absurd that we have to do this – we're a rock'n'roll band. But Sellafield 2 increases radiation by 1,000 per cent. Someone has to do something. *On taking part in a demonstration against a British nuclear power plant in Sellafield, Cumbria, August 1992*

Sellafield 2 will be an environmental disaster, and it would appear that it is also an economic disaster. The Germans are considering pulling out, even the British government is considering pulling out. They've spent two billion pounds of British taxpayers' money on Sellafield 2 already. It will take another billion to see it through. We are asking the people of Britain to stop and think, to take this seriously, as it affects us all. We have a chance for the first time right now to impress upon the British government the madness of opening Sellafield 2. *January 1993*

I think one of the most shocking things was for me to find out I didn't know the facts. I didn't know that the Irish sea was the most radioactive stretch of sea in the world. It is absurd that a rock'n'roll band such as this had to do anything to bring the facts out. 1993

The Future

We haven't made the record that we want to make yet. And we're going to, one day, and that's really where we are right now. And I'm telling you, this is not the band of the Eighties. We're just getting it together, just about. *October 1988*

We do intend to clog up the airwaves for some time to come. Y'know, the sorta mega album then the mega silence is just too much of a cliché at this point. You know, we put out the record and then we tour it around the world for a year and a half, and then we go to Barbados and have a holiday for another year and a half, and then we come back. That's so boring. U2 are on a sort of suicidal kind of... not physically but musically... we intend to make music until people are sick of us. We just don't care at this point! We've nothing to lose! *November 1988*

As long as the records keep getting better, we'll keep together. As soon as they get worse, I'm off. *April 1992*

We're just as serious about what we do now. We're just pretending not to be. *May 1992*

I've decided U2 can go in two extremes. We use the studio like an instrument, mesh into it, smash it, manipulate it – we drop acid on it. Or we go into a room with the basics, guitars, a violin, and record in five minutes. Most bands make the mistake of being in the middle. They'll do a drum track for days and all they're doing is making death music. It has no life whatsoever.

There is this curve in rock'n'roll, where a lot of people do their best work in the first ten years, and then, it's on – they're on cruise control, if they do stay together. But I don't see why that has to be. I mean, it's not true of poets or playwrights, or other writers. I mean there's no real reason for that. It just happens to have been the way. I'm expecting that, you know, we're going to get a whole lot better at being able to – realise – the songs we hear in our head. Which have always been, for me, much more interesting than the ones I hear on our records. *February 1992*